The Complete Book of
CROSS-COUNTRY
SKIING
and
SKI TOURING

The Complete Book of
CROSS-COUNTRY SKIING
and
SKI TOURING

ARTHUR LIEBERS

COWARD, McCANN & GEOGHEGAN, INC.
NEW YORK

CONTENTS

The Complete Book of
CROSS-COUNTRY
SKIING
and
SKI TOURING

INTRODUCTION

Ski tourers enjoy a jaunt through the woods—one of the
differences between Alpine and Nordic skiing.
Killington, Vermont photo by Bob Perry

The last ten years have witnessed a considerable change in the American and Canadian ski world. Since the early thirties, when skiing began to develop as a winter sport, the emphasis had been on Alpine skiing—the downhill running aspect of the sport. More and more technical skill was devoted to creating new mechanical devices to get skiers up the slopes easily so that they could make the downhill run and then be pulled or lifted up the slope for more downhill runs. Skiing equipment and techniques followed this pattern. An unpleasant concomitant of this development was an extremely high accident rate. It takes no skill to ride a mechanical device up a hill; it does take some to get down in one piece.

The relative affluence of recent years and the increased leisure time found more and more people flocking to the ski slopes. The resulting population boom in the ski resort areas meant longer and longer waits at the ski lifts and traffic jams on the roads to winter resorts; the urban sprawl reached the snow areas.

There have always been some purists in the ski world who have followed the traditional pattern of skiing—using skis as a means of getting from one place to another over the snow. In Europe, particularly in the Scandinavian countries, recreational

One way to get the whole family on the ski trail, even if one of its members is too young to handle his (or her) own skis.
Elizabeth Presnikoff photo, Stowe, Vermont

ski touring and cross-country racing were the winter sports of both young and old. As more and more Americans followed this trend, beginning in 1960, the face of skiing began to change, and Americans began to realize the particular pleasures and advantages of ski touring:

THE UNIVERSAL WINTER SPORT

• There is no "right" age for enjoying ski touring, nor any required physical condition. Anyone who can walk can learn the walk-ski touring movements. Like walking, ski touring has rightly been described as a lifetime activity. Tots, teens, middle-aged, retired—all can participate in ski touring.

• In many parts of the United States and Canada, hikers, hunters, and fishermen can ski tour in winter over the same terrain that they cover in summer. With proper touring equipment and basic ski-touring technique, they travel over snow far faster and easier than on foot or on snowshoes.

• In recent years, many Alpine skiers have discovered that ski touring adds a new dimension to their sport. This is especially true for the urban skiers, who often flee city streets only to stand on long lift lines on weekends. In ski touring, they find a pleasant change.

• Athletes have found that cross-country ski racing is the most demanding of all endurance events and the most comprehensive of all skiing events. In the Olympics and the Fédération Internationale de Ski, there are twelve Nordic events, just double the number of Alpine events. Of these twelve, ten involve cross-country racing and seven are pure cross-country racing: 15-kilometer, 30-kilometer, and 50-kilometer: individual races for men; 5-kilometer and 10-kilometer individual races for women; 4 X 10-kilometer relay race for men, and 3 X 5-kilometer relay races for women. Others involve cross-country racing with ski jumping, and the Biathlon combines cross-country racing and rifle shooting.

• There is no ski-touring equivalent for the "golf widow." It is a sport that can be enjoyed by the entire family. A backyard or a playground becomes a ski area for tots, who can learn touring skiing not long after they have learned to walk. A park or golf course is an ideal winter playground for youngsters— and their elders—on touring skis.

• Most of all, Nordic ski touring is ideal for the adult beginner who understandably may be cautious about taking up Alpine skiing because of its cost, its danger, as reflected in the statistics of Alpine-skiing accidents, and the difficulty of acquiring sufficient skill to perform Alpine skiing with relaxed enjoyment.

• Ski touring has also been found an ideal recreation for the handicapped, who may find other winter sports difficult, if not impossible. In Norway, the annual *Ridderrennet* (Race of the Knights) cross-country race week attracts blind and disabled skiers from all over the world. The *Ridderrennet* is partially supported by the International Association of Lions Club, and a number of Americans, supported by their local Lions Clubs, have entered the races, some of them having been beginners on skis.

• The hardier and more adventurous combine ski touring with winter camping, exploration, and mountaineering.

While ski touring can be learned on a do-it-yourself basis, most beginners will find that a few hours of instruction make the learning process much easier. The recent upswing in ski touring in North America has resulted in an amazing increase in the number of marked trails and ski-touring facilities (described in later sections of this book). Also, many Alpine ski areas now offer marked trails, equipment rental, and instruction classes for the touring skier. In addition, the various divisions of the United States Ski Association and the Canadian Amateur Ski Association have touring programs and touring facilities.

Sources of information for the ski tourer are:

United States Ski Association
1726 Champa Street
Denver, Colorado 80202

14

The two faces of ski touring: *Above,* solitude and new-
fallen snow; *below,* the popular Engadin Ski Marathon,
a yearly event at Majola, Switzerland.

Canadian Amateur Ski Association
PO Box 2566
Station D
Ottawa, Ontario

Ski Touring Association
Box 9
West Simsbury, Connecticut 06092

THE SKI TOURING COUNCIL

The Ski Touring Council, a noncommercial membership committee, was formed in 1962, with the purpose of reviving the then almost-forgotten sport of ski touring, and can justly lay claim to having given this activity its impetus in the United States.

In one of its bulletins, the council clearly states the basic appeal of ski touring:

Anyone of sound wind and limb, capable of enjoying the dazzling beauty of a crisp, clear winter day in the country, can indulge in the pleasure of ski touring. Little skill is required and very little expense is involved. All that is needed is a light snow cover and trails. The trails may be hikers' summer trails, unused dirt roads, bridle paths or even golf links. The ski tourer may set his own pace and roam far from crowds—taking in the delights of woodland, fields, hills and mountains. Closely related to cross-country skiing which aims at perfection of performance and speed, the ski tourer will aim to acquire sufficient skill to fully enjoy this purely non-competitive recreational activity.

Small outlay covers touring skis (From $20 to $45), bindings ($6 to $10), poles ($6 to $14), touring boots ($25 to $35). A complete set of children's skis, binding and poles ($13 to $28). A pair of knickers or jeans, socks, sweater, a parka and mittens will complete the outfit. Clothing should not be too heavy because the exercise of ski touring warms the whole body.

Each winter, the council arranges guided touring trips and workshops in Connecticut, Maine, Massachusetts, New Hampshire, New Jersey, New York, Pennsylvania, and Vermont. During the fall, several preconditioning hiking trips are held. All tours are graded for novices, intermediates, and experts. They are one-day tours, held either on Saturday or Sunday. Each February, an overnight camping tour is held.

The workshops teach all essentials of ski touring, are especially aimed at beginners, and are usually held over weekends.

All tours and workshops are open to all comers and are free of charge. The areas hosting the workshops usually charge a small registration fee of about $2. The schedule of workshops containing dates and details is usually available from the council by about the middle of September, for a $2 charge.

In its activities, the Ski Touring Council works closely with the U.S. Amateur Ski Association, the Nordic Ski Patrol System, the Metropolitan New York Ski Council, and with outdoor organizations such as the Adirondacks Mountain Club, the Appalachian Mountain Club, the Green Mountain Club, the White Mountain Association, and American Youth Hostels.

The annual publication of the council, its *Ski Touring Guide*, is available for $1.75 and includes general information on ski touring, detailed information on layout and marking of ski touring trails, equipment, waxing, ski-touring technique, how to arrange ski-touring trips and necessary safety measures, and a list of ski-touring trails in the eastern United States.

This is available from the Ski Touring Council, West Hill Road, Troy, Vermont 05868.

To order its publications or for further details on the council, contact one of the following:

COLORADO

U.S. Amateur Ski Association
1726 Champa Street
Denver, Colorado 80202

17

MASSACHUSETTS

Appalachian Mountain Club
5 Joy Street
Boston, Massachusetts 02108

Gordon Spencer
322 Oak Street
Westwood, Massachusetts 02090
Phone 617-769-0527 (Evenings before ten)

Nordic Ski Patrol System
David P. Hodgdon, Director
29 Westwood Terrace
Dedham, Massachusetts 02026

ILLINOIS

American Youth Hostels, Inc.
3712 North Clark Street
Chicago, Illinois 60613

NEW HAMPSHIRE

White Mountain Association
Box T
Lancaster, New Hampshire 03584

NEW YORK

Adirondack Mountain Club
R.D. 1
Ridge Road,
Glen Falls, New York 12841

Almy D. Coggeshall
414 Oak Ridge Drive
Schenectady, New York 12306
Phone 518-377-2305

George Froelich, Vice Chairman
Ski Touring Committee of the U.S.
Eastern Amateur Ski Association
51-01 39th Avenue
Long Island City, New York

Metropolitan New York Ski Council
415 Madison Avenue
New York, New York 10017

VERMONT

Green Mountain Club
PO Box 94
Rutland, Vermont 05701

Ski Touring Council
R.F. Mattesich, President
West Hill Road
Troy, Vermont 05868
Phone 802-744-2472

THE NORDIC SKI TOURING PATROL

The volunteer members of the National Ski Patrol are a familiar sight on many Alpine skiing slopes, where they try to instill a message of safety into recreational skiers—and to rescue those who did not get the message. Within the last two years, the Nordic Ski Touring Patrol has been organized to render the same service to ski tourers on the more popular trails.

Most active in the eastern United States, the patrol has been able to participate in about a third of the trips sponsored by the Ski Touring Council and has sent patrollers out with the Sierra Club, the MIT Outing Club, and the New Jersey Ski Council.

More members are being sought. The basic requirement is at least intermediate ski-touring ability, knowledge of ski-touring technique and equipment, and possession of a current advanced Red Cross card.

Through the patrol, candidates for membership can participate in workshops in such areas as winter camping, survival camping, skiing, and use of the toboggan.

Information on regular and associate membership in the patrol is available from:

David P. Hodgdon, Director
Eastern Division, National Ski Patrol
29 Westwood Terrace
Dedham, Massachusetts 02026

PART I
History

Ski touring in Jotunheimen, Norway's famous "Home of the Giants." Here, a view of the Skagastøl peaks.
Courtesy Norwegian National Tourist Office

1

WHERE IT BEGAN–
NORWAY

Norway can well lay claim to be the motherland of skiing. In that country skis have long been the winter mode of travel, and the recreational and sports aspects of ski touring and cross-country competition are a part of the country's tradition.

For Norwegians, skiing runs in the blood: The tradition can be traced back four thousand years. Heel straps found not far south of the Polar Circle, and ancient skis found in boggy ground show that even in prehistoric times the design of skis had reached a high level.

On the other hand, even as late as the middle of the last century, the actual technique of skiing was still only relatively poorly developed. This was the fault not of the skis, but of the bindings, which, since they consisted only of a toe strap, made steering next to impossible. Indeed, skiing then was no more than a caricature of what we would nowadays think of as real skiing. The skier would just run slowly down a small hill, carrying an enormous brake pole which was supposed to be of help at crucial moments.

But then came skiers from the county of Telemark, Norway, with their epoch-making invention—bindings that went tight round the heel, so that the skier's feet were securely fastened.

With this binding it now became possible to turn with skis and even to jump. From now on the skier could, in theory, steer his skis, and not the other way around, as was more often the case earlier.

Modern skiing, then, has only been in existence for the last hundred years, four thousand years having been spent on the preceding technical developments! Now, however, things began to move quite fast. Ski clubs were founded, contests were organized, and after a few decades the whole of Norway seemed to be skiing.

But only Norway. It is remarkable, in fact, that while skis have been used in Norway for an inconceivably long time, they were still completely unknown elsewhere. In the newspapers of the day we find reports of more than fifty skiing contests, with almost 4,000 active participants. In practice, this must mean that almost one hundred years ago there were about 40,000 to 50,000 Norwegians who went skiing, and at a time when the word "ski" was hardly known in the world outside.

The first tales of the Norwegians and their skiing to spread abroad concerned their achievements in ski jumping. With astonishment people in central Europe read that the Norwegians could fly many meters through the air, with a pair of "wings of wood, fastened to the feet." Many held these to be wild, fantastic stories of some Baron Munchausen. When these stories were rejected, it was because such a "sport" concerned only the inhabitants of the North, the neighbors of the North Pole, and could not possibly have any relevance to people in southern countries. While they perhaps gave credit to these fabulous stories, though without concerning themselves unduly with them, they themselves might be stumbling about their areas up to their knees in dry, fine snow, perhaps occasionally with crude snowshoes on their feet. When there was an unusually heavy snowfall, farmhouses in the Alps might stay as isolated islands for months at a time without being able to establish contact with their neighbors, all because one of the simplest means of loco- motion in existence—skis—was still lacking.

Ski touring begins on a main street in Norway. A view from the center of Lillehammer, a well-known Norwegian ski resort.

Courtesy Norwegian National Tourist Office

After the ski binding enclosing the heel had been "invented" in Telemark, and demonstrations in the capital (then called Christiania, now Oslo) had shown that skiing was a most pleasant recreation for the long winter months, a whole army of skiers soon appeared. In fact, in a very short time skiing became the national sport of the Norwegians, equally popular in all circles. The reason for this can be readily appreciated if one looks at the skis actually used nowadays by various sections of the population. Comparing the skis left outside a luxury cottage in the mountains with those standing outside the wall of a small-holder's home in the lowlands, one finds no marked differences. A wealthy man may own a luxury villa or a car or sailing boat in the highest price range, but when it comes to skis, the poor are as well equipped as the rich. Skis, in other words, are the most democratic form of winter transportation for Norwegians, owned and, as it were, tended with love by the entire population. People in other countries have coined phrases reflecting this fact: "The Norwegians are born with skis on their feet," or, "Norway is the home of the skier," and so on.

Even the foundations of skiing in Austria can be traced back to Norway. In 1888 the polar explorer Fridtjof Nansen accomplished the feat of traversing the Greenland icecap, where no man had ever before gone on skis; and his subsequent account of his trip, published in 1890, caused a great sensation. His realistic descriptions of his adventures, published fortnightly in yellow papercovers, were devoured by readers everywhere.

In German, the story was entitled *Auf Schneeschuhen durch Grönland*, since the word "ski" was unknown and would not have been understood by readers from the Alpine countries. Nevertheless, Nansen's book gave many Austrians the desire to own a pair of those "magic boards," which could apparently carry people securely across the snow and down precipices with lightning speed, and even lead one through the air like a bird. Meanwhile, in 1889, an Austrian from Graz, named Max Kleineschek, who had, some nine years earlier, started a correspondence with a Norwegian from Trondheim in order to exchange postage stamps, had already inquired in one of his letters whether one might also use skis in the Alps and had received a positive answer. And so interest in the sport was aroused, though only slowly at first. Only when Norwegians went to Austria in the early 1890's did things really begin to happen.

A young Norwegian, W. B. Samson, was at that time a baker's apprentice in Vienna. As winter began and the snow started falling, he had a pair of skis sent from home. Whenever he had these on, either in the parks of Vienna or elsewhere, a crowd of curious onlookers always gathered. One day he wanted to demonstrate his skill in ski jumping. He heaped up snow on a mound in a park until it took on the shape of a ski jump and was then able to float through the air for a whole 6 meters, while his Austrian audience watched in astonishment. Today, of course, it seems strange that seventy-five years ago—and indeed even later —the Norwegians should have been so far superior to skiers of all other nations, for there is no denying that of late the pupils have overtaken their master. In the winter of 1967, for instance, it was an Austrian who registered the world's longest ski jump with a jump of 154 meters in the Vikersund competition. And although the Norwegians for years took pride in exporting the best skis obtainable anywhere, they themselves today often buy Austrian slalom skis.

Indeed, all that really remains of the old Norwegian influence in Austria and the rest of the world, as far as skiing is concerned, is the terminology. The Norwegian word *ski* and terms like *slalom, Telemark-turn*, and *Christiania-turn* (christie) are common to the whole world. But for all that, relatively few people know that slalom really means a ski track down a slope (*sla*-slope and *lom*-track) and originates in Telemark—or even that the "christie," more fully known as the "Christiania-turn," is so called because it originated in Christiania, where the term was first introduced in 1900. But it was natives of Telemark who, a hundred years ago, first turned with parallel skis, after they had developed real ski bindings.

At the end of the last century, even before competitions had started in earnest, skis were a commonplace feature of day-to-day winter life in Norway and an indispensable means of communication throughout the country. They were used for hunting in the mountains and in the forests and for fishing in winter from the small mountain lakes. At times when a new baby was expected, the midwife often had to strap on her skis. Doctors had to go on skis for miles to give help to people taken ill. The country priest often had to put on skis to reach his church on a cold Sunday morning, and the congregations likewise. Even as recently as fifty to sixty years ago, it still sometimes happened that it was only by the help of this simple means of transport that members of Parliament could reach the capital. In short, all groups of the population were dependent on skis. Every village and every valley had its special type of ski, peculiar to that district. In Osterdalen, a peculiar type was developed. On the left foot one had a long ski—up to 3 meters or even longer—and on the right foot a short ski of about 2.2 meters, covered in fur, with which one pushed while sliding on the longer ski. It was not easy to replace these skis; an indication of their value is seen in the fact that in one case which occurred in the eighteenth century, a man's property was so divided that one son got a milking cow while the other got a pair of Osterdals skis.

From these different types of skis the best kinds were developed, and the skis used in Telemark were the best of all. These skis were about 8 centimeters wide at the front and about 6.8 centimeters wide at the middle, where the bindings were fastened. At the back they again became broader, though not as broad as at the front—about 7.4 centimeters. It was found that such skis with curving edges consistently won in competition with other types, and this today is the dominant pattern for skis everywhere in the world, whether for slalom, long-distance racing, or jumping. Skis, indeed, are a commodity which has changed very little in the course of time. If one today measures a ski at the front, in the middle, or at the back, one still finds the same proportions that the farmers in Telemark had already adopted by the middle of the last century.

They start them young in Norway. Here, a photo from
the Geilo Ski School at Geilo, a popular ski resort.
Courtesy Norwegian National Tourist Office

To talk in this way, however, about "farmers in Telemark" is
not altogether accurate. It was in fact a single man from
Morgedal, in Telemark, who developed this type of ski, and it
was also he who first made the binding go around the heel and
thus created modern skiing. His name was Sondre Norheim, and
he really is the father of skiing as we know it, having initiated
both ski jumping and slalom. Nevertheless, he himself earned
nothing from his "invention," and he died poor and unknown in
America, to which he had emigrated at the age of fifty-nine. It
was also he who in his youth first made skiing into a really
exciting sport. When he rushed down the steep slopes of Morge-

dal and jumped the hillocks, uttering his Red Indian war cry, the other boys were quite wild with enthusiasm. They gathered around him and sought to emulate his achievements, which, from all we have heard about them, must have been unique, for he was a born virtuoso and equilibrist on skis. When, in 1868, he went (by ski of course) from Morgedal to Christiania to participate in a competition, he proved by far the ablest man present. The combination of his native ability and his new bindings made the other competitors look like beginners, although he was by then already forty-five years old. It was this competition in Christiania which really established the modern idea of pleasure skiing. Now life came to the slopes: people began charging about on their skis, jumping and running slalom, laughing and enjoying themselves, regardless of whether they managed to stand when they jumped. If one fell, it was quite common to have to go back up the hill in order to "raise the woman," which meant that one had to make it down the hill without falling. This expression still survives everywhere in Norway. "To raise the woman" was more than just a phrase; it was a principle, and one which made a good foundation for a skier who could hold his own in any situation, however great the speed and however difficult the jump.

Today it is common in Norway to give children skis for Christmas when they are between four and five years old, and if snow conditions are good, the little ones will be on the slopes with their parents even on Christmas Day. Nor does it take long before parents and children will be out together on much longer skiing trips, too. It is typically Norwegian to take cross-country ski trips lasting several hours, coming home to a meal prepared in advance and to lively conversation about the events of the day.

It is not all remarkable, in fact, on any average weekend, to see whole families out skiing together, and at Easter, most Norwegians take ten days off in mountain cottages and hotels in order to enjoy the sun. Easter, indeed, has become the most popular holiday of the year, and one must book well in advance in

Skiing is a family affair in Norway, where children are "born with skiis on," and even toddlers go along on outings.
Courtesy Norwegian National Tourist Office

order to get accommodation in tourist cottages, hotels, or boardinghouses.

Every self-respecting factory, large office, school, or business arranges an annual skiing competition sometime during the winter. After the race, the prize giving takes place at a small party. In hotels, too, it is common to arrange races. So that everyone has a chance to participate, there is usually a long-distance race for those who have mastered neither jumping nor slalom, in which the competitors decide their own time, each registering before the start how long he thinks he will spend. If the course is 3 kilometers long, for instance, one skier might put

The annual "Birkebeiner" race in Norway. The route covers thirty-five miles from Lillehammer to Rena and is based on the historical route followed by two Vikings more than 700 years ago, when they carried the infant prince, Hakon Hakonson, to safety.

Courtesy of the Norwegian National Tourist Office

himself down for twenty-five minutes, another for ten minutes, and a third who is not so fast, for forty-two minutes. The one who obtains the time closest to his own guess has won the race. These so-called reliability races are very popular; both sexes have the same chance of winning, and a Sunday skier can compete on equal terms with a racing expert.

In order to promote skiing (as if this were necessary in the home of skiers), special badges have been introduced in the last few years for those who cover long distances. One has to have skied 250 kilometers in order to obtain the badge in gold. Thousands make an effort to fulfill these conditions, and the best skiers are not satisfied with 500 kilometers. There are many who in a good skiing season cover a distance of more than 2,000 kilometers—farther than the distance from Oslo to Vienna!

The ordinary skiing badge also induces many people to get out on their skis. In order to obtain this, one has to cover a distance of 10 (or 5) kilometers in a certain specified time. There are various grades of badge: In the first year, one can get the badge in bronze, then the next badge in silver, then enamel, and, finally, the gold badge. Even when one has achieved one badge by the end of a season, there will still be enough left for the future.

While the use of skis for travel and sport developed in Norway and the other Scandinavian countries, skiing followed other paths in the United States. In the early 1930's skiing first began to gain popularity in this country, but it was Alpine skiing— downhill running—that caught on. This trend led to the development of ski equipment specifically for the Alpine sport, tows and lifts in every winter-sports area, to meet this demand, and teaching of techniques for downhill running. Only within the last decade has cross-crountry skiing and ski touring achieved a tremendous growth of interest among recreational and competitive skiers. However, because of their long lead in this activity, foreigners dominate the competitive cross-country (Nordic) events in the Olympics and other international meets. American competitors have hardly ever placed in important meets.

PART II

The Basics of Ski Touring

2

EQUIPMENT

Nordic ski touring can be defined as "a biped activity on skis." It is very much like walking on foot and, like walking, has many variations.

Biped activity is a general term covering many activities such as strolling, hiking, jogging, running, toddling, and so on. Different footwear is required for each of these activities: street shoes, hiking boots, tennis shoes, track shoes, children's shoes, and other types. These categories do not mix well. Hiking boots are as out of place for a stroll in the park as street shoes are for a mountain climb.

Nordic ski touring, the accepted skier's term for cross-country skiing, is also a general term. It includes many different types of locomotion such as mountaineering, hiking, light touring, jogging, or children's toddling. As in footwear, there are different types of Nordic ski-touring equipment to match each kind of activity.

To simplify the equipment dilemma, ski-touring equipment is available in four categories to match the four general types of ski-touring activity:

General touring equipment is for all-around ski touring, including stronger equipment designed for ski mountaineering.

Light touring equipment is lighter than general touring equipment. It can be used for strolling or serious touring. In the

Scandinavian countries, it is the most popular type of equipment.

Cross-country equipment is the lightest category and is designed for the jogger and racer. The specialized racing equipment in this group can be used safely only on prepared cross-country racing tracks.

Children's equipment is lightweight, simple, and inexpensive, and is intended for tots up to the five-year-olds. Older children are best provided with children's sizes of the three types just described.

ALPINE AND NORDIC EQUIPMENT

There are substantial differences between Alpine and Nordic equipment. Alpine equipment, which has dominated the ski world in recent years, has been designed for the skier who is hoisted up a slope by some mechanical device and then skis down. Nordic equipment is specially designed for the do-it-yourself skier who depends on his skis to get him where he is headed—and back.

The major dimensions and weights of the various types of Nordic skis, boots, and bindings are compared with their Alpine counterparts in the Equipment Comparison Table on page 39. Children's equipment which is specialized to a single age group is not included in the table. The weights listed in the column to the far right reflect the major difference between Nordic ski-touring equipment and Alpine equipment—the Nordic is far lighter. The old adage "a pound on your feet is like five on your back" helps explain the effortless grace of the cross-country skier.

It is recommended that Nordic ski-touring equipment be selected according to its planned use, with consideration to individual size, skiing ability, frequency of use, and budget.

NORDIC TOURING SKIS

The most apparent variation among the different types of Nordic touring skis is in their width, as measured at the narrowest point, approximately at the middle of the ski.

Cross-country skis are the lightest of all Nordic skis and are recommended for jogging, training, and racing. Their widths are approximately $1\frac{7}{8}$ inches. Racing skis often have hollow channels or balsawood center laminations to reduce weight. However, this also reduces their strength and limits their effective use to prepared cross-country racing racks.

Light touring skis resemble the cross-country types, but are sturdier and slightly heavier. Their widths range up to approximately $1\frac{31}{32}$ inches. They are intended for use by recreational touring skiers.

General touring skis are designed for all-around use. Their widths are approximately $2\frac{1}{32}$ inches and wider. The wider general touring skis are easier to turn on downhill runs than light touring or cross-country skis. Some heavier and wider (widths of $2\frac{1}{8}$ inches and wider) general touring skis are called mountain skis, as they are intended for ski mountaineering, where tracks must be broken continually and skiers may be carrying heavy packs on steep terrain.

All Nordic touring skis have softer tips and stiffer tails to give the forward spring that is characteristic of the touring stride. Skis are made of wood and fiberglass in various combinations. Wooden skis dominate the field. As many as seven different woods, in thirty to thirty-six laminations, are used in wooden skis, with the wood types and number of laminations determining the characteristics of the ski, its weight for a given size, and its price. For example, hickory is one of the strongest woods available for laminations, but it is also the heaviest and most expensive. A considerable amount of American hickory has been exported from the United States to the Scandinavian and other ski-manufacturing countries. Ash, on the other hand, is lighter, springier, and cheaper than hickory, but it is also far weaker.

The most common types of fiberglass skis are made of fiberglass top and bottom laminations on a laminated wood core, or with "wet-wrap" construction involving epoxy-impregnated fiberglass wrapped around a core of laminated wood or expanded plastic.

Skis Example: 205 cm (6 foot, 9 inch) skis				Boots Example: Men's 41 (US:9)		Bindings		Total weight of skis, boots and bindings
Type	Edges	Min. width	Pair weight	Features	Pair weight	Type	Pair weight	
Cross-Country Racing	hardwood or plastic	1-7/8 in.	2 lb 11 oz.	light, flexible cut below ankle resemble ordinary shoes	1 lb 10 oz	cross-country toe clamp	5 oz	4 lb 10 oz - 5 lb
Cross-Country Training & Jogging	hardwood, plastic, or compressed hardwood	1-7/8 in.	3 lb 12 oz.					5 lb 11 oz
Light Touring	compressed hardwood, or plastic	1-31/32 in.	4 lb 7 oz.	Similar to above, cut above ankle	2 lb			6 lb 12 oz
General Touring	compressed hardwood, plastic, or aluminium	2-1/32 in.	5 lb 8 oz.	resembles hiking boot	3 lb 9 oz	toe-iron with heelcable or band	2 lb 2 oz	11 lb 3 oz
Alpine fiberglass	steel	2-1/4 in.	10 lb.	double, plastic with buckles	8 lb 13 oz	toe-release with heel release	2 lb 13 oz	21 lb 10 oz
Alpine metal	steel	2-1/4 in.	11 lb.					22 lb 10 oz

Equipment Comparsion Table

With similar characteristics, a laminated wood ski is the cheapest; the fiberglass on wood-core laminated skis, and the wet-wrap fiberglass skis are respectively more costly.

Most touring skis must be waxed, but a few "waxless" models are on the market. The "waxless" characteristic is achieved by a pair of mohair strips set in the base of the ski with the hair facing backward. This strip arrangement works in this same manner as the furs used on skis by Alpine ski climbers (climbing furs).

In selecting the proper touring ski, the ski length and camber (arch) should be considered in accord with your height, weight, and skiing ability.

Lengths of Nordic touring skis are determined by the same general principles as the Alpine skis, with three notable exceptions:

(1) Nordic skis are longer than the corresponding Alpine skis because the thinner skis need extra length to have enough bottom area for stability and grip and glide in the touring stride.

(2) Apart from children's skis, there are no short or GLM (graduated length method) skis recommended for touring.

(3) The camber of a pair of Nordic skis is greater than that of a pair of Alpine skis of the same length. This is because a touring ski must both grip and glide on the snow, and not just glide as does an Alpine ski. Flattening the camber against the snow is one of the mechanisms that produces grip.

The Proper Touring-Ski Length

The lengths of touring skis are measured along the sole of the ski from its tip to its tail and thus are longer than direct-line lengths from tip to tail. For instance, a 210-centimeter touring ski will measure 207 centimeters in a direct line from tip to tail.

The *Length Selection Diagram* shown here indicates the ski length for persons of average body build. Lighter-than-average skiers may use slightly shorter skis, while heavier-than-average skiers may use slightly longer ones. As a general rule, a woman's

Length Guide for Nordic Skis and Poles
Children's, women's and men's ski lengths and pole lengths are selected according to height. The ski lengths given here are for persons of average build. Those who are heavier or lighter than the average should use ski length slightly longer or slightly shorter, respectively, than those listed in the table.

CHILDREN

Height ft.	in.	Ski Length centimeters	Pole Length centimeters	Inches
3'	4"	120	poles not recommended for	
3'	7"	130	children under 4 ft. tall	
3'	9"	140		
4'	0"	150	90	35
4'	2"	160	95	37
4'	5"	170	100	39
4'	7"	180	105	41
4'	9"	185	105	43
4'	11"	190	110	45
5'	1"	195	115	47
5'	4"	195	120	41
5'	6"	200	125	49

WOMEN

Height ft.	in.	Ski Length centimeters	Pole Length centimeters	Inches
4'	9"	185	110	43
4'	11"	185	115	45
5'	1"	190	120	47
5'	3"	190	125	49
5'	5"	195	130	51
5'	7"	200	135	53
5'	9"	205	140	55

MEN

Height ft.	in.	Ski Length centimeters	Pole Length centimeters	Inches
5'	1"	195	120	47
5'	3"	200	125	49
5'	5"	205	130	51
5'	7"	210	135	53
5'	9"	210	140	55
5'	11"	210	145	57
6'	1"	215	150	59
6'	3"	220	155	61

skis should be approximately 5 centimeters shorter than those for a man of the same height, weight, and skiing ability. Serious touring skiers and cross-country ski racers who have above-average skiing ability and desire to ski faster will generally select lengths slightly greater than those suggested in the diagram.

Skis for growing children should be selected on the basis of body height alone, without regard to sex or weight. This is because children's-size skis, especially among the better brands, are essentially scaled-down adult models and are extremely strong for their length. A length equaling the measurement from the floor to the fingertips of a child standing with his arm extended vertically will be approximately correct and will be suitable for use over a two- or three-year period.

The Important Camber of the Ski

There is no general rule for finding a ski with the proper camber for the individual. Generally, the heavier or more skillful the skier, the stiffer and thus greater the camber. Active cross-country racers often have several pairs of skis with varying camber. "Soft" camber skis are preferable for soft tracks; "hard" or greater camber skis for hard tracks.

The camber of laminated wooden skis may change with age and use; this may explain why Nordic touring skis are seldom calibrated in camber or stiffness at the factory. A ski that has absorbed moisture by being left in the snow or being stored in a damp place will lose camber. A ski that has been subjected to dry heat will gain camber. Because of these conditions, it is almost impossible to provide an easy guide to camber selection. As a general rule, if your weight on a ski on the shop floor will not flatten out the camber, then the ski is probably too stiff.

The camber of a ski can be altered slightly to suit individual needs. To decrease camber, you can tie a pair of skis together at the middle and let them stand for a few days. To increase camber, gently heat the skis on their tops with a waxing torch, tie together the tips and tails, and let stand to cool. Never block

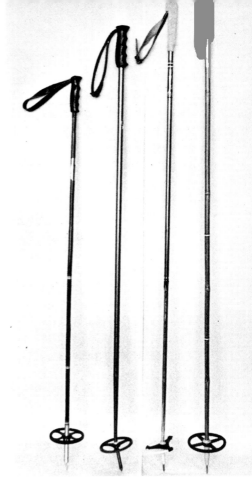

The Poles: Four lightweight cross-country ski poles are shown here. Three to the left are metal, the fourth is bamboo (tonkin). The bend in the tip of the North American Nordic pole (second from left) is there to make it easier to get the pole in and out of the snow.
Elizabeth Presnikoff photo for The Knowlton & McCleary Company

laminated touring skis. Blocking does not successfully increase or preserve camber, but rather alters the camber curve by distorting tip and tail. This ruins the desired relationship between the gripping ability of the skis and their gliding ability.

THE POLES

Nordic touring poles should be springier, or more "lively," than Alpine poles. This is because they are not simply planted in the snow as an aid to turning or for balance, but, rather, are planted, pulled on, and pushed on in the various phases of the touring strides. Their lively shafts provide a little "whip" which helps push the skier forward much as does the forward-spring characteristic of the touring skis. Nordic pole grips have tapered elliptical cross sections but no finger recesses as do Alpine poles, because they must suit the many different hand positions used in touring. Nordic pole tips are set at an angle to the shaft. This is because the poles are rarely planted with a straight-down movement as are Alpine poles, but are generally swung forward and into the snow. The pole tips angle or curve forward to help the pole snag on the snow in planting and to facilitate pole withdrawal.

The Nordic poles traditionally have been made of treated bamboo—tonkin cane—which has the desired combination of light weight, liveliness, and strength. Fiberglass poles and metal poles are now manufactured with these characteristics. Generally, tonkin poles are the cheapest, while fiberglass poles and metal poles are stronger for their weight.

Grips

Grips are made of molded plastic or leather. The molded grips are cheaper and well suited to general touring, while the leather ones give better friction to the hand in its various positions on the pole. Straps are made of leather and may be either one-piece or adjustable.

The "baskets" are plastic or metal rings fixed to the pole shaft by plastic or rubber webs.

Outwardly, there is little difference among general touring, light touring, and cross-country racing poles. As a general rule, the faster the skier, the livelier the pole. Baskets on general touring poles are about 4½ to 5 inches in diameter. Cross-country racing pole baskets are smaller, about 3½ inches in diameter, as these poles are made for use on packed cross-country racing tracks, and the smaller diameter saves weight.

Choosing the Pole Length

The Length-Guide Table provides general information for selecting the pole to suit you. For a more personal fit, choose the pole length by standing with feet together on a flat surface, wearing ordinary low-heeled street shoes. A vertical pole, with its tip on the floor at your side, should reach to just above the armpit for general touring use and fit snugly under the armpit for light touring and cross-country racing. This slight difference in length is due to the fact that the jogger or racer will have a slightly more pronounced forward lean and a slightly deeper crouch in the diagonal stride than the general touring skier.

Nordic poles are made in lengths of 75 to 120 centimeters for children, and 120 to 160 centimeters for adults, in increments of 5 centimeters for general and light touring, and 2.5 centimeters for racing.

TOURING BINDINGS

Ski touring requires that the heel be free to lift off the ski, so Nordic bindings attach to the boot at the toe only. Bindings are classified according to how this toe-only attachment is achieved. The two types are:

Toe bindings, in which the attachment mechanism is included in the toepiece, and

Cable or *strap bindings*, in which the boot is held in place in the toepiece by pressure from a cable or a strap around the boot heel.

In general practice, toe bindings are preferred for light touring and cross-country, while the cable or strap bindings are used for general touring and for mountain skiing.

Kinds of Toe Bindings

Several kinds of toe bindings are available. All have the common characteristic that the boot is attached only by the tip of the boot sole. There are three general types:

Peg bindings are those in which a clamp presses the welt of the boot sole down against two or three pegs projecting upward from the toepiece and which fit into the recesses in the sole.

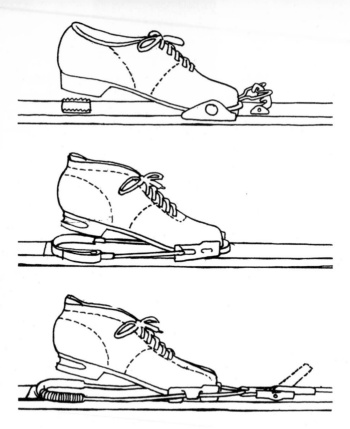

Ski-tour bindings: *Top,* toe binding; *center,* strap binding; *bottom,* cable binding.

Silva, Inc. photo

Spike bindings are those in which two spikelike pegs mate with recesses or go through holes in either side of the sole welt.

Step-in bindings have a spring-loaded catch in the toepiece which fits a toepiece attachment on the boot.

Most toe bindings are available only in three or four fixed widths, generally one for children and three for adults. This is possible because the manufacturers have standardized their product. All boots and bindings have standard side angles (14 degrees outside and 8.5 degrees inside), and binding size is simply selected to match boot size. Most bindings mount with three or four screws.

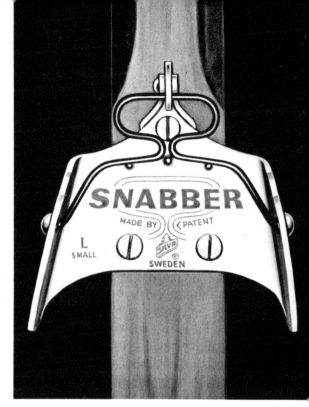

Among the simplest types of touring bindings is the Snabber, which holds the toe of the boot firmly against the three vertical pins on the toeplate.
Silva, Inc. photo

Cross-country cable binding with toe lugs adjustable for sole thickness, and telescopic lever.
Silva, Inc. photo

Some binding manufacturers offer a mounting jig for correct placement and predrilling screwholes for the binding.

The cable or strap bindings use pressure against the heel to hold the toe in place. The cable binding comprises a toepiece, a cable with a heel spring, and a front throw for tightening the cable. This type of binding can also be provided with side hitches to hold the heels down for downhill skiing. This type of binding is not recommended for beginners, as the foot is fastened securely to the ski with neither a release mechanism nor the free-twisting "automatic safety" of the toe binding.

The strap binding is somewhat simpler, consisting of a toepiece and a metal strap running around the boot heel with a ratchet type of clamp for tightening.

Mounting the Bindings

Mounting the bindings on the skis calls for some expertise and should be done by a professional, if possible. Touring bindings should be mounted with the toe of the boot approximately over the ski's balance point. The ski, with its binding attached, should drop downward at the tip when lifted by the center of the binding ears. The idea behind this is that the ski when lifted in use will drop slightly in the diagonal touring stride and the tip of the ski will stay in contact with the snow.

One problem in touring is that the boots are supple and may twist horizontally when held only by their toes. Heel plates are available to prevent a weighted boot heel from slipping off the ski to the side. The plates are mounted on the ski, right under the heel, and consist of serrated or flexible metal, plastic, or rubber devices that either dig into the boot heel or provide a high-friction contact with the heel. Some heel plates are in the form of a raised metal piece which mates with a corresponding recess in the boot heel.

TOURING BOOTS

Touring boots are quite unlike the cumbersome and heavy

Typical lightweight touring boot in a three-pin binding. This one is a North American Nordic boot manufactured in the United States.

Elizabeth Presnikoff photo for The Knowlton & Mcleary Company

The racing and touring boot is higher. The vulcanized sole is predrilled to fit pins of the Rotefella type of bindings. The most popular touring binding, the Rotefella uses three pins to hold the sole of the boot, and the front clamp is on the same piece of hardware as the toe socket, reducing the number of screws necessary to hold the binding to the ski. On this boot the heel is grooved to accommodate cable bindings.

Silva, Inc. photo

Alpine ski boots and come in four different types to match the four types of Nordic touring skis:

General touring boots resemble hiking boots. They are cut above the ankle, are generally padded or semipadded, and have a double or sealed-tongue arrangement to keep the boot watertight.

Light touring boots are cut at the ankle and resemble men's street shoes. Most light touring boots have a cable groove in the heel so that they may be used with cable- or strap types of bindings.

Cross-country boots are similar to the light touring boots, but are cut below the ankle. Sole width at the instep, heel size, and sole thickness are all minimum to cut down on weight.

Children's boots generally resemble general touring boots, which give some support to the ankle, and should be fitted to the correct size of the child's foot. Avoid buying a larger size and padding it with socks, hoping that the user will grow up to it the next season or two.

Leather boots are the most popular, although a few models of rubber light touring boots lined with synthetic fleece are available. Soles are usually laminated leather topped by a textured rubber sheet or, in some modern styles, polyurethane-vulcanized to the uppers. The vulcanized sole has the advantage of sealing the boot and fixing the sole shape, which is better for mounting. The leather-rubber sandwich sole is slightly more flexible and can be repaired using conventional shoe-repair machines.

BASE PREPARATION AND WAXING

In downhill skiing, technique is the mystique of the sport; in Nordic skiing, waxing is the mystique. New Nordic skiers and those who convert from the Alpine sport are amazed to find that the same wax can make your skis cling to the snow while climbing uphill or touring and then make them slide faster downhill.

However, the outer layer of wax—the running wax—cannot be applied to the bare bottoms of the skis. The first step in preparing your skis for use is to apply a base preparation to which the running wax will adhere. The base covering also protects the ski from moisture. You might note that there are some skis available which have epoxy-impregnated laminate bottoms or special bottom coatings which require no base preparation. If so, these skis will be so marked.

Base Preparation

The first step in preparing a wooden-base ski is to remove the protective coating which has been applied at the factory. The dealer can advise you which solvent to use to remove this finish. The next step is to apply some sort of pine-tar compound over the entire bottom of the ski. Here the situation becomes a bit complicated.

The professional and the most effective way of getting the base surface onto the ski is to heat the pine tar into the ski, using the butane torch that is part of the Nordic skier's standard equipment. Place a thin layer of tar over the bottom of the ski, and keep the flame of the torch moving fairly rapidly. Use a rag to wipe off the excess tar, which should bubble slightly as it is being heated. The completed job should be a smooth layer of the bottom compound, which should feel slightly tacky when dry.

If the burning-in process seems frightening, you can get a satisfactory base for normal touring by using an impregnating compound which resembles creosote. It is brushed or sprayed on ski bottoms and dries in about eight to twelve hours.

Waxing

Which wax to use and when probably accounts for more conversation and controversy than any other aspect of Nordic skiing. The proper wax to use at any given time is determined by the type of snow, and this in turn is affected by the air temperature at any given time. The wax selected must serve a dual purpose. It must be soft enough to grip the snow when the ski is weighted and at rest and, at the same time, be hard enough so that when the ski is in motion, it will move over the surface of

The next step: Rubbing in the wax that he hopes will produce the best results on the day's snow.
U.S. Army photo

A U.S. Biathlon team member prepares his skis by burning-in the base compound.
U.S. Army photo

the snow. If the ski is improperly waxed, it will slide too much and cause loss of control or stick to the snow with such emphasis that you will hardly be able to move.

Most manufacturers offer a full line of about ten types of wax, and the avid cross-country racer will carry a full complement in his kit. However, these are the different basic types of wax:

Hard waxes come in round cans and are recommended for temperatures below freezing. (Note that imported waxes are marked in centigrade rather than Fahrenheit readings, and that 0 centigrade is the freezing point.)

Klister waxes are tacky, hard waxes, also come in round cans, and are generally used for temperatures at and above freezing.

Klisters are thick fluids, come in tubes, and are used for temperatures above freezing and over ice or crusty snow.

The average recreational skier should be able to manage well enough with three waxes—one each of the basic types. Recently, Bass Sports has come out with what it calls the American Waxing System, with red, white, and blue waxes. The red is suggested for warm snow (above-freezing air temperature), the blue for cold dry snow, and the white for crusty, refrozen snow.

The hard waxes are usually rubbed on and smoothed out with the cork that comes with the can. The klisters are squeezed out of the tube and spread in a thin layer with a metal scraper. However, for a better job, both these types can be "torched" in for a smoother finish.

Here are some general hints on waxing. For best results, waxing should be done indoors at room temperature, although it can be done outdoors, especially when it becomes necessary to change the wax during a tour. Allow the wax to harden by cooling awhile before skiing. Skis should always be cleaned of old wax before you apply a new coat.

If there is a question about which type of wax to use, choose a harder wax. You can always apply a softer wax on top of a harder one, but not the reverse.

By trial and error, you will be able to find out how thick a layer of wax to apply. Generally, a thin layer will do for a few hours of skiing; a longer tour will call for a heavier deposit on your skis. In applying the wax, several thin layers superimposed are more lasting than one thick layer.

Give your wax a chance before giving up on it. It takes a few hundred yards of travel for a new layer of wax to "run in" and begin working properly.

One of the insider's tricks in waxing is to use a combination of waxes. Place a harder wax on the tips and tails of your skis and a softer wax under the boot. This should give you extra grip for climbing.

Perhaps the best advice about waxing is to follow the manufacturer's instructions. As a rule, the color codes used by the different companies represent fairly similar waxes, and one company's red, or green, or blue will be pretty much like another's.

Finally, if you are not a perfectionist, you can use the lazy man's system and try some of the aerosol spray waxes that seem to meet the needs of the beginner.

CLOTHING TIPS

Touring is a far more energetic sport than Alpine skiing, so ski clothing for touring is different from that worn by the Alpine skier.

Since the touring skier moves more and generates more body heat than the Alpine skier, his clothing must allow for ventilation, yet be warm and wind-resistant. Like Alpine ski clothing, it must also be water-repellent.

A single- or double-shell parka, or *anorak*, in the Norwegian terminology of cross-country, over a woolen shirt or sweater is adequate for most ski-touring needs.

Knickers and knee socks are best for touring because they allow for complete knee freedom in the various touring strides. Alpine ski stretch pants are not recommended for touring, as they offer extra resistance for the legs to overcome in striding. Single- or double-poplin knickers are the most suitable for general touring, while light-touring skiers and cross-country racers seem to prefer double-knit nylon stretch knickers. For ski mountaineering, loose full-length ski pants or overpants over knickers are preferred.

Matching sets of double-knit nylon or poplin knickers and blouse or *anorak* are available in a wide range of colors and designs and are widely advertised in the skiing magazines and to some extent in the high-fashion publications.

Caps, gloves, and mittens are as necessary as they are in Alpine skiing but are preferably much lighter than those which would be used for Alpine skiing under the same weather conditions.

Rucksacks for the Touring Skier

The ski tourer needs a pack on his back to carry food and beverages and the useful miscellaneous equipment which will be discussed in the following paragraphs.

The Norwegian types of rucksacks have been developed especially for skiing. They are light, allow full arm movement, and place the weight carried close to the back, where it will not unbalance the skier on downhill runs or turns.

The Norwegian frame rucksack is specially designed for ski touring and is available in a variety of models and sizes. Generally, a frame rucksack has one or two inner compartments and one to three outside pockets.

Modern rucksack frames are made of aluminum or aluminum alloys, and the packs are made of nylon or nylon-cotton duck fabric.

Pack sizes vary from small day packs to larger semi-packboard rucksacks. Most touring skiers will find the smaller day pack adequate for their needs.

Two Suggested Accessories

In addition to the food and beverages in the touring skier's pack and the waxes and waxing equipment, two other pieces of miscellaneous equipment may come in handy:

Spare ski tips. If touring skis break, they usually break at the tip, so a spare tip is advisable for longer tours. Most spare tips are simply aluminum or plastic tip-shaped pieces which force-fit or tie onto a broken ski, just back of the break.

Pullover socks of double-knit nylon terry cloth or nylon-rubber go over light-touring or cross-country boots to keep them warm and dry in extreme weather.

Cross-country ski racers and serious touring skiers can keep in shape for skiing by following a year-round training program. Because skiing is very much like walking, training for touring is very much like training for running. But because touring uses both the arms and the legs, touring training differs from running training in that it also involves developing the arm muscles.

Elastic cords or friction-loaded cords are used for maintaining the strength of the arm muscles used in the various touring strides. (A full program of training for the competitive cross-country skier is given in Chapter 4.)

Roller skis are a popular training device. As their name implies, they are skis on wheels or rollers. Generally, they consist of short aluminum platforms with one to three wheels with tires. One or two of the wheels are fitted with ratchets to keep the skis from moving backward. Toe bindings are mounted so that the foot is positioned midway between the front and back wheels, and light-touring or cross-country boots are used. The skis are intended for use on gentle uphill stretches of asphalt or other hard surfaces, not for going downhill, as they have no brakes. The touring diagonal stride and the double-pole stride can be done on roller skis much as they are down on snow, thus enabling skiers to simulate skiing when there is no snow. Roller skis have become so popular in Norway that roller-ski races are held in the summertime as off-season competition for cross-country racers.

A similar device, a small, wheeled platform for indoor home use is available from SKIMATIC, Box 2193, Livonia, Michigan 48151.

CARE OF THE TOURING EQUIPMENT

Wax on skis hardens in time and becomes difficult to remove.

Skis should be cleaned and base-treated (if necessary) before storage. Paraffin can be used to seal any top surface scratches. The general rule for storage is to keep moisture out, as nothing ruins skis more quickly than absorbed moisture. Touring skis should be stored in a cool, dry place. Modern laminating methods have elminated the need for tying skis together, for blocking, or for special storage positions. Properly base-treated touring skis can simply be stood in a corner until the next season.

During the ski season, skis should be base-treated as often as necessary, which is whenever a bit of bare wood shows. Most recreational skiers need base-treat their skis only once or twice a year. Care of skis with synthetic soles should follow the manufacturer's recommendations.

Check binding screws for tightness periodically during the ski season and before storage.

Ski-touring boots may be treated with the same polishes and wax type of waterproofing compounds as are used for hiking boots. Waterproofing greases should not be used, as they make the leather excessively pliable and allow it to stretch out of shape.

Most touring-pole tips are screw-in types which can be replaced when dulled, although some tips are large enough to allow several sharpenings. Straps, grips, and basket attachments should be checked at least once a year.

EQUIPMENT CHECKLIST

When you are out on the ski trail, it is too late to think of what you should have brought along, but did not. The following checklist may help you avoid that situation:

Clothing

Long underwear
Cotton shirt or turtleneck
Wool shirt or ski sweater
Nylon wind shirt, or outer wind parka

Ski pants or knickers
Socks, heavy wool and light cotton (extra set)
Ski cap
Bandanna or scarf
Dark glasses or goggles
Gloves or mittens (chosen according to temperature expected)
Watch

Ski Gear

Boots
Skis and bindings
Poles
Waxing kit or climbing skins

Accessories

Day pack or rucksack
Emergency repair kit for skis
First-aid kit
Sunburn protection for face and lips
Water canteen or flask
Food for trail snacks or lunch
Map and compass, if required
Avalanche cord

Extra Gear for Snow Camping

Large rucksack or back carrier
Sleeping bag
Plastic cup or bowl
Eating utensils
Après-ski booties or overboots
Headlamp or flashlight and extra batteries
Waterproof matches
Toilet kit
Proper food and liquids

Good striding technique, basic to ski touring, is demonstrated by two Swiss cross-country skiers.
Courtesy Swiss National Tourist Office

3

BASIC SKI-TOURING TECHNIQUE

Ski touring is a natural activity which is fairly easily learned to the point where it can be truly enjoyed. This is because it is basically nothing more than a variation of walking, which we can all do. So basic is the connection between walking and touring skiing that, for example, the Norwegians have no word for skiing. They simply say *gå på ski*, literally, "walk on skis."

Your problem as a beginning touring skier is to forget that you have skis on your feet. Once you can manage to forget about the skis and start walking as you do on foot, you are more than halfway to mastering the basic touring diagonal stride.

THE DIAGONAL STRIDE

The diagonal stride means that the opposite arm and leg work together, just as in walking. The movement of a good diagonal stride resembles an exaggerated march step in which the arms and legs swing forward and back.

The diagonal stride is perhaps best learned by simply walking on skis on the flat. Make all movements as walklike as possible.

Increasing the push with each step, leaning the upper body a bit more forward, and swinging the arms a bit more in a march-like manner will produce the correct diagonal stride. As in walk-

61

ing, the push of each foot is what propels you forward. The poles, planted in the snow when your arm is in front of your body and released as your arm swings back of your body, are only a help. The poles supply only about one-fifth of the energy needed to drive you forward.

As the push of each step increases, the force will be enough to propel you forward, gliding on the opposite ski. The stronger the push, the longer the glide. This gliding phase is the essential and perhaps the only real difference between walking, and touring on skis.

A skilled touring skier's diagonal stride has short, rapid push-offs or "kicks," alternated with long glides. "Kick, glide—kick, glide" is the working order for touring movements. It really does not look too much like walking, which is probably why a number of complicated theories and systems have been advanced to teach the diagonal glide. Or perhaps walking is really not that simple. It's just that when most of us learned to walk, we were not old enough to read any instructions on how to walk. Like babies learning to walk, walkers learn to ski tour simply by moving as a biped.

UPHILL AND DOWNHILL

The Difference Is Uphill

Uphills are what really make touring skiing vastly different from Alpine skiing. Touring skiers must get uphill under their own power, while Alpine skiers can ride.

The Diagonal Stride.

Ski touring is international. Here, the gliding exercise is being taught at a Swiss cross-country school.

Courtesy Swiss National Tourist Office

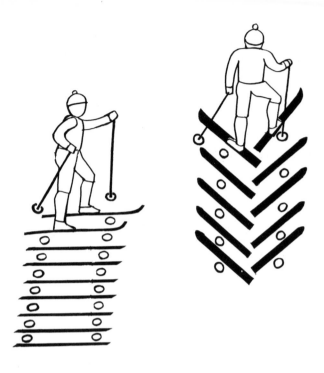

Getting uphill: the herringbone (left) and the sidestep.

For gentle uphills, the ordinary diagonal stride will do. As in walking uphill, you must lean a bit into the hill and shorten your stride a bit.

For steeper hills, ski upward on successive traverses linked by kick turns or stepped tacking turns. For still steeper hills or for going up the fall line, use herringbone or sidestepping.

The *herringbone* is a sort of reverse snowplow. When you find that you are losing your grip when trying to progress straight up a slope, spread your ski tips in a wide V. Then dish the skis inward on their edges, and keep walking straight up. Use your poles behind you as props. You will probably find this an exhausting way to get up a hill, and it is practical only for fairly short distances. If you look behind as you struggle up a slope

64

The Kick Turn.

this way, you will see how this technique got its name, from the pattern of tracks it leaves on the snow.

An alternative to the herringbone is the *sidestep*, also shown in the sketches. This maneuver is fairly obvious. Just place your skis horizontally across the slope. Rolling your knees and ankles slightly inward will give you a grip on the lower edges of your skis. Then you can work your way up the slope. While sidestepping takes relatively little effort, it is nonetheless a very slow way of climbing.

The *traverse* means moving on a diagonal across the slope, gaining some altitude on each leg. Basically, the maneuver resembles tacking in sailing. At the end of each leg you reverse your direction by stopping and using the stationary *kick turn*. This turn is used to make a 180 degree turn in place. Practice this turn first on a flat place. The idea is to support yourself solidly on your poles. Then lift the poles one at a time to get the skis around them. The sketch will give you an idea of this turn, which is simpler than it sounds.

The Step Turn.

The *stepped turn* is not very graceful and will not mark you as an accomplished ski tourer, but it is a simple way for the beginner to get himself facing in another direction. Try it on a level place where you will not have to use your poles for support. Place all your weight on one ski, and lift the other at a divergent angle, toward the direction you want to go. Then transfer your weight to that ski, lift the other ski, and place it parallel to the one you moved. Repeat this process until you are facing in the desired direction. You can also use this turn to change direction when you are skiing down a gentle slope at low speed.

Downhill Is Different, Too

Nordic touring equipment is freer, more flexible, and much lighter than Alpine equipment. This means that the entire body is used more in skiing downhill and in turning than if you were using Alpine equipment.

Downhill strategy: The skier on the left is "braking." The one on the right is following the "fall line" downhill.

Elizabeth Presnikoff photo, Stowe, Vermont

At Stowe, Vermont, a gentle slope gives the tourer a chance to let gravity help him along his route.

Elizabeth Presnikoff photo,
Stowe, Vermont

The wide-track downhill position is both technically and physiologically correct for the touring skier, as it is the position of natural readiness and balance. The downhill running stances are the same as those used in Alpine skiing, varying from the more erect natural stance to the high-speed "egg position." Since touring bindings allow heel freedom, the whole foot is weighted in skiing downhill.

The *snowplow* is the basic running technique for downhill skiing, and is well adapted to the beginner. The skis are kept fairly widely apart at the backs and close together in front. By bending the knees and pressing down on the inner edges of the skis, it is possible to keep good control and move at a fairly slow pace. You will also find that the snowplow allows easy turns. For example, if you want to turn to the left, "weigh" your right ski by putting your body weight on it, and slightly lift your left ski. You will find yourself moving to the left. Reverse the procedure to change direction to the right. This is the basic idea of stem turns.

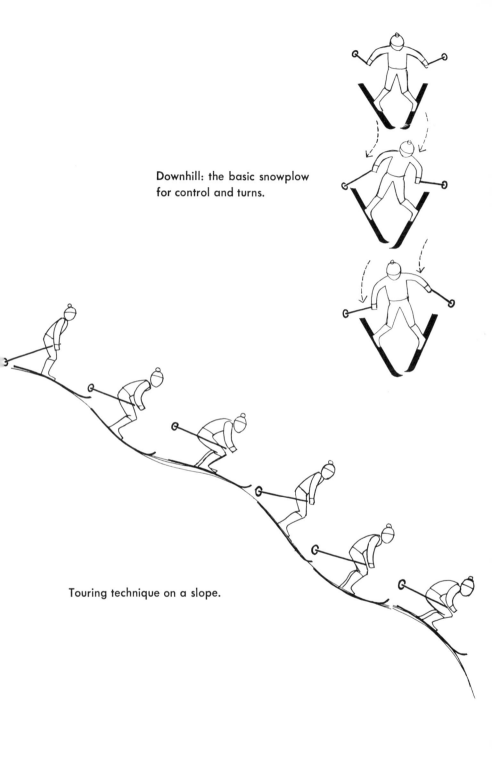

Downhill: the basic snowplow for control and turns.

Touring technique on a slope.

Gripping the pole.

To get a bit more speed down a slope, bring the skis closer together as you gain more confidence in your ability to remain upright.

Downhill skiing is regulated as it is in Alpine skiing by doing linked turns or snowplowing. The wide-track downhill stance lends itself easily to the standard stem turn, which is touring's most-used turn. The snowplow, or double-stem turn, is slightly more stable than the stem turn and is a good turn for beginners. Skilled touring skiers prefer stem-Christianias or parallel turns. Expert touring skiers and racers can do tightly linked parallel turns or even *wedeln* on cross-country racing equipment.

USE OF THE POLES

Use of the poles in Nordic skiing is fairly simple. You will find that after you have planted your poles and begun the forward kick with your ski, your arm will react naturally, pushing backward. In no time at all, you should fall into the pattern of pushing backward as the diagonally opposing ski goes forward. Your natural impulse to retain your balance will come into play, regulating the relationship between the skis and the poles.

Use of the pole should be completely relaxed. Even when you are thrusting with the pole, your grip on the handle should be

Note the use of the poles to keep forward momentum on
a gentle uphill slope.
Courtesy Swiss National Tourist Office

These two cross-country skiers are using their poles to gain more speed on a down-slope run.

Courtesy Swiss National Tourist Office

firm but not tense. When your arm reaches the vertical point, about halfway in your swing, you should loosen your grip. As soon as the pole stops pushing forcefully backward, relax your grip. At the farthest point behind you, you should be holding the pole very loosely.

Bringing the pole forward should soon become a part of the natural cadence of your stride over the snow. Once the pole is released from the snow, its pendulum action will tend to carry it forward. As it swings forward, gather it into your hand, trying not to clasp it too firmly. Even during the power thrust that helps you move forward, the strap that holds the pole to your wrist carries a lot of strain and reduces the need for a too-tight grip on the handle.

One tip on poling: Try to keep the pole from swinging too far forward. It should be planted at just about where your feet are. If the pole goes well beyond your boots, pushing down on it will have a slowing effect on your forward momentum. In correct use, the pole should always be pointed slightly toward the back.

OTHER ELEMENTS OF SKI TOURING

On the flat or on slight downhills, *double-poling* alone or combined with striding replaces the diagonal stride. Double-poling is simply planting the poles, sinking weight-over, and then pushing on both poles simultaneously while gliding on equally weighted skis. It is used to gain speed on good tracks or on downhill stretches. However, it takes a great deal more energy than the diagonal stride and cannot be maintained for any long period of time.

Double-pole striding sounds a bit more complicated in the explanation than it is in practice. It combines the leg movements of the diagonal stride with the double-poling arm movements. The push-off or kick is timed to be completed as the arms are swung fully forward for planting the poles. The stride can be accomplished with two kicks, the second one occurring just as the poles are planted.

The *passgang*, or lateral striding, means that the arm and the leg on one side work together. When the right arm is forward, the right leg is forward, and so on. The passgang is the opposite of the diagonal stride and was the accepted technique in the days when skiers used only one pole. However, modern understanding of ski technique has shown the passgang to be inefficient, energy-wasting, and unnatural to learn. It is extremely difficult to run passgang on foot, so why do it on skis? It can be done for fun, but not as a serious part of technique.

Another "fun" technique in touring is to use a skating technique with your skis. The skating or step turn is one of the common flat or downhill turns in touring.

Preliminary exercises to warm up the muscles before starting out on a cross-country jaunt.

Courtesy Swiss National Tourist Office

4

PHYSICAL CONDITIONING FOR CROSS-COUNTRY SKIING

While it is true that almost everyone who can walk can ski tour, there will be a greater enjoyment in the sport if one is in good enough physical condition to do a bit more than just tread along on his skis.

The conditioning exercises on the following pages are the result of considerable research by the U.S. Army and are used in preparing competitors for the Biathlon competition in international and Olympic tournaments. This regime is planned for the serious cross-country competitor. The reader interested in recreational touring may find that just using the first thirteen exercises will be enough to get him in trim for a winter's activity on skis.

If you are one of those who find it difficult to engage in solitary calisthenics, almost any form of "endurance" outdoor activity can get you in condition for the ski trail.

Trainers suggest that jogging, rugged hiking, long-distance canoeing, or an outdoor job that calls for manual effort can condition your body.

CALISTHENICS

Calisthenics are an essential part of the cross-country and

Biathlon training program, affording coordination and conditioning for all parts of the body. There are various types of calisthenics. Sessions begin with fifteen to thirty minutes of running and twenty to thirty minutes of exercises. Working continuously without benefit of rest will give you the best results. Consistent participation is essential. As training increases with ease of movement, one may add more exercises and increase his tempo. If you are not used to exercise, start more gradually and work up to this schedule.

Benefits of Exercise. The benefits of exercise are not always understood, but here are some of the more important ones:

• Muscular tone is improved, flabbiness prevented, and, at the same time, muscular strength and endurance are built up.

• Circulo-respiratory endurance is improved through a process of opening up dormant lung capacity to absorb greater amounts of oxygen.

• Circulation of the blood is speeded up and extended to a greater portion of the body as the force exerted by exercise forces the blood to service all parts of the body. The efficiency and effectiveness of the heart, lungs, and blood vessels are improved.

• Flexibility is maintained. This provides a wider range of movement and the ability to accomplish a greater number of physical skills with rapidity.

• Elimination of body wastes is regulated and assisted by the bending and twisting of the body and the general speedup of body processes.

• Tension is relieved through the working off of excess nervous energy and in the loss of daily worries and cares.

• Sleep is improved because muscles are healthfully tired after training. A by-product of sound sleep is relief of tension.

• Control of obesity is made possible by the burning of excessive amounts of fat-producing food elements.

• Susceptibility to injury is reduced by maintaining muscular tone through exercise. Injuries such as hernia and back strain are less likely to occur if muscles are maintained in proper tone.

Deep-breathing Rhythm. Correct breathing is one of the most important factors in effective exercising. Deep breathing in a proper rhythm should be developed.

Deep breathing stimulates the heart action, improves the diaphragm, and makes it easier to bring oxygen into the body and pump out carbon dioxide. More blood is carried by the capillaries to muscle fibers, feeding them the nutrients for strength.

Good breathing rhythms will aid in the development of your chest and improve your breath control.

The objective of the following exercises is to condition all major muscles of the body and to provide variety to the conditioning program.

No. 1. STATIONARY WALK. Walk, keeping feet in place. This exercise is used to loosen up the leg and arm muscles. (2 minutes)

No. 2. BODY BEND. The feet are spread, arms overhead, elbows locked. Bend at the waist, swing arms down to touch the floor. Recover to the starting position with a sharp and vigorous movement. (20 times)

No. 3. TOE RISES. Feet together, swing arms forward and upward to a full stretch overhead and at the same time rise high on the toes. Swing the arms sideward and downward slowly. (50 times)

No. 4. KNEE PULL. Raise the right knee up. With both hands pull knee to chest. Recover and raise the left knee and repeat the same procedure. (20 times and repeat)

No. 5. ARMSWING. Feet spread, right foot a half step forward. Bend forward at the waist and swing the left hand to the right foot and the right hand overhead. Then swing the right hand to the left foot, left hand overhead. (20 times and repeat)

No. 6. NECK ROLL. Feet apart, hands on hips. Bend the head forward with chin on chest and roll head to the right, back, left, and to the front. (10 times and repeat)

No. 7. BACK BENDER. Feet apart, fingers laced behind the head. Bend the upper trunk backward, raising the chest high, pulling the elbows back and looking upward. Keep the knees straight. Recover to the starting position. (20 times)

1
Stationary
Walk

2
Body Bend

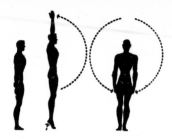

3
Toe Raises

4
Knee Pull

5
Arm Swing
(Bend Position)

6
Neck Roll

7
Back Bend

8
Side Straddle Hop

9
Full Squatter

10
Ski Poling
Arm Swing

11
Push-up

12
Shoulder Stretch

13
Side Kick

14
Ski Kick

15
Stomach Stretch

16
Rocker

17
Sitting Arm Swing

18
*Ankle Pull
Back Stretch*

19
Sit-ups

20
Bicycle

21
Scissor

22
Forward Bend

23
Squat Jump

24
Side Bend

25
*Stationary
Run*

Courtesy U.S. Army Modern Winter Biathlon Training Center

No. 8. SIDE-STRADDLE HOP. From the position of attention, jump, spreading the feet and swinging the arms sideward and overhead. Jump, bring the feet together, swinging the arms down to the side. (2 minutes)

No. 9. FULL SQUATTER. Feet together, hands on hips, assume a full knee bend. Recover to the starting position. (20 times)

No. 10. SKI POLE ARM SWING. Feet slightly apart, bend body forward at the waist. Swing the arms as in ski poling. (20 times and repeat)

No. 11. PUSH-UPS. From the front leaning rest position. Toes and heels are together and the body is straight from head to heel. Lower the body, keeping it straight until the chest touches the ground then raise the body until the elbows are locked. (20-plus times)

No. 12. SHOULDER STRETCH. Kneel on the ground with the trunk bent forward, arms extended over the head resting on the ground. Push down from the shoulders stretching the shoulders and back muscles. (20 times)

No. 13. SIDE KICK. Squat, placing the hands on the ground about one foot in front of the feet. Kick the right leg to the side, recover. Kick the left leg to the side and recover. (2 minutes)

No. 14. SKI KICK. Front leaning rest position. With right knee on the ground. Bend the left knee and bring the left foot as far forward as possible, then kick to the rear. Repeat three or four times, then alternate and do the same with the right leg (20 times and repeat)

No. 15. STOMACH STRETCH. Front leaning rest position. Relax, sagging the back but keeping the elbows locked, stretching the stomach muscles. (20 times)

No. 16. ROCKER. In the prone position, clasp the hands behind the back, arch the body, holding the head back. Start rocking, using the front part of the trunk as a rocker. (1 minute and repeat)

No. 17. SITTING ARM SWING. Seated on the ground, feet apart, arms sideward at shoulder level, palms up. Turn trunk to the right as far as possible, recover slightly; then repeat, recover, turn trunk to the left as far as possible. Recover slightly then repeat. Recover. (20 times and repeat)

No. 18. BACK STRETCH. Seated on the ground, legs slightly apart, hands grasping the lower part of the legs. Bend forward, bobbing down and touching the head to the right knee and the left knee. Recover; then repeat. (20 times and repeat)

No. 19. SIT-UPS. From the back position with the fingers laced behind the head, sit up, bend forward, touching the right elbow to the left knee, return to the back position, repeat, touching the left elbow to the right knee. (20 times and repeat)

No. 20. BICYCLE. From the back position, raise the legs and hips. Keep the elbows on the ground, and support the hips with the hands. Move the legs vigorously as if pedaling a bicycle. (1 minute)

No. 21. BACK POSITION SCISSORS. From the back position raise the legs and hips. Keep the elbows on the ground and support the hips with the hands. Move the legs in a scissors kick. (20 times and repeat)

No. 22. FORWARD BEND. Feet apart, fingers laced behind the head. Bend forward as far as possible, keeping the knees locked. Recover slightly, bend forward as far as possible, and recover. (20 times)

No. 23. LUNGE. Feet apart, hands on hips. Lunge forward with the left foot, maintaining the trunk erect and hands remaining on hips, elbows back. Recover slightly, and repeat. Recover sharply to starting position. Repeat the action, reversing the feet, and continue alternating. (2 minutes)

No. 24. SIDE BENDER AND HIP ROLL. The feet are spread more than shoulder width. A wide base is required. The arms are raised overhead. The thumbs are interlocked and the elbows locked. Bend to the left as far as possible, roll hips in circular motion counterclockwise, then recover sharply to the starting position. Then bend to the right as far as possible, recover slightly, and again bend to the right as far as possible and roll hip in circular motion clockwise. Recover sharply to the starting position. (20 times and repeat)

No. 25. STATIONARY RUN. Run on the balls and toes of the feet, raise the knees high, keep the back straight, and swing the arms to the front and rear. (2 minutes)

EXERCISES WITH WEIGHTS

To build up strength in your whole body, concentrate on correcting your weakest points. Work speedily, and stretch out with each weight exercise. Occasionally you can increase the weights some. In this program, always start with some limbering-up exercises and with some relaxing exercises. Be thoroughly warmed up before starting the lifting.

1. CURL (regular underhand grip). Stand erect, holding weight suspended at arm's length. Bring the weight in a semi-circular path up to shoulder level, keeping elbows at sides. The back is kept straight; don't allow yourself to bend backward or move your elbows back. Develops arms, shoulders, and upper back.

2. PRESS BEHIND NECK. With the barbell resting on your shoulders against the back of your neck, press the bar up to arm's length overhead; then lower to the starting position. Keep the knees and back straight. This press, in addition to building the triceps and shoulders, will develop the important trapezius muscle of the upper back.

3. UPRIGHT ROWING. Keep your legs and back straight. Pull the weight straight up to the neck. Elbows are kept out wide, away from the body. Lower barbell to straight-arm position. Develops lower arms, shoulders, and back muscles.

4. FORWARD OVERHEAD RISE. Stand with feet apart, bar resting on the thighs. Raise the bar in a slow, controlled movement straight forward with elbows locked and up and overhead. Return bar slowly to the starting position, resisting the weight with the shoulders and arms. Develops the shoulders, back, and chest muscles.

5. PULLOVER. In the supine position, with the bar resting on the thighs, lift in a slow, controlled, semicircular movement over the head, keeping the arms straight, elbows locked. Reverse the

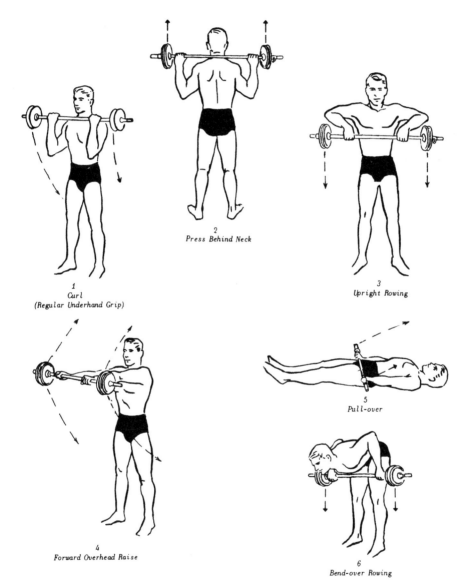

1
Curl
(Regular Underhand Grip)

2
Press Behind Neck

3
Upright Rowing

4
Forward Overhead Raise

5
Pull-over

6
Bend-over Rowing

7
Sit-ups

8
Side Bend

9
Forward Bend

10
Squats

11
Toe Raise

Courtesy U.S. Army Modern Winter Biathlon Training Center

movement back to the starting position. This develops the chest and back muscles.

6. BEND-OVER ROWING. Stand with feet apart. Bend at the waist so that the upper body is parallel to the ground, supporting bar in straight-arm position. Keep legs and back straight. Pull the weight straight up to the neck, using arms and shoulders to do all the work. Elbows are kept out wide, away from the body. Next, lower bar to straight-arm position. This develops shoulders, back, and wing muscles.

7. SIT-UPS. Lie flat on your back with your feet anchored under anything heavy enough to hold them down. With the bar across the chest, raise up to the sitting position, keeping the back straight. Return to the starting position, slowly resisting movement with your stomach tensed. This exercise develops the back, stomach, and legs.

8. SIDE BEND. Place the bar across your shoulders, behind your neck, bend to one side as far as possible, then to the other side, and return to starting position. Don't bend your knees or allow yourself to bend forward. All the work should be done at the waist. Side bending is important in developing a strong trunk.

9. FORWARD BEND. Stand with feet apart, trunk erect, bar across shoulders. Bend forward to the waist so that upper body is parallel to the ground. Keep back and legs straight. Then return to the standing position. Develops the abdominal, back, and side muscles.

10. SQUATS. Place the bar of the barbell against the back of your neck, and squat down, making sure to keep your head up and your back perfectly straight; then return to the standing position. Squats will develop powerful legs, chest, and lung capacity.

11. TOE RAISE. Stand erect, feet apart, barbell overhead. Keeping your back and legs straight, slowly raise up as high as possible on your toes; then return to standing position. Do half of the exercises with the toes pointed out and the other half with the toes pointed in. This develops both parts of the two-headed calf muscles.

PART III
The Ski-Tour Camper

One of nature's tricks with trees and snow is a bonus on a ski-touring trip.
Courtesy Crested Butte, Colorado

5

COMBINING
SKI TOURING AND
WINTER CAMPING

Winter camping is a logical development of ski touring. For generations, the Scandinavians and other European ski tourers have extended their trips beyond one day by camping outdoors. However, the Scandinavian ski trails and those in the Alps enjoy a profusion of overnight huts and camping shelters; usually three-walled, roofed shelters with rude bunks that provide a comfortable nesting place for the skier in his sleeping bag and that can be warmed to some extent by a fire kept going all night just in front of the hut.

However, there are still not too many of these shelters available in the United States. A number of state parks and some of the national parks do have shelters along hiking trails that could be used in the winter by the ski tourer. A letter to the National Park Service in Washington, D.C., or to the department of parks or conservation in your state capital máy bring you information on shelters that could be used in the winter. Also, organizations such as the Dartmouth Outdoor Club, the Appalachian Mountain Club, and hiking clubs in various parts of the country maintain such shelters.

For the ski tourer or the ski-touring family that would enjoy trips of more than one day, but that views sleeping outdoors with some apprehension, there are a number of alternatives. Most camping trailers and mobile campers are fitted with an adequate heating apparatus, and many have reported successful use of the VW camper-bus as a winter home-away-from-home. In using these vehicles, care should be taken to provide some ventilation to prevent any buildup of dangerous fumes in the closed vehicle, although most heaters are vented to provide protection.

For off-highway winter use, the towing vehicle should have adequate traction—a four-wheel drive is almost a must, as are proper snow tires or chains, shovels for emergency use, and a towrope or chain of adequate strength.

For the hardier types who plan to carry their sleeping accommodations on their backs, the chapter on safety discusses some of the situations that the winter camper may face and how to meet them. The "survival" sleeping setups described there also provide camp shelters for one-night bivouacs in the snow.

Snow camping in winter requires sturdier equipment than that used on one-day tours. The weight of the pack which will carry extra clothing, sleeping bag, probably a tent, food and cooking utensils, first-aid kit, and other essentials, means that travel will be far slower for the camper than for the unencumbered skier. The downhill runs will of necessity be much more restrained, and climbing skins may be necessary to get uphill with the addiional weight.

THE SLEEPING BAG

The first essential element for comfort and safety when spending the night outdoors is a sleeping bag. The Sierra Club, which has had much experience in this field, suggests that a fairly light-weight bag is adequate for anything except the most rigorous arctic conditions. In today's market, a satisfactory, down-filled bag should run a bit over $75. Lightweight nylon, the 1.9-ounce type, has been found most satisfactory and offers the advantage that nylon "breathes" to some extent. The cotton outer covering may be a little cheaper, although it is somewhat heavier.

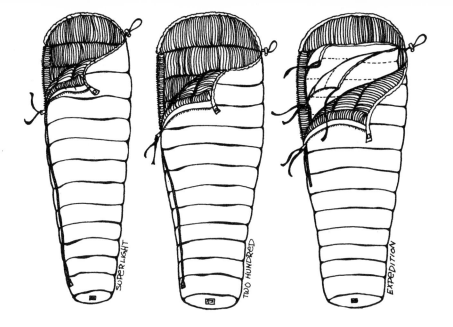

Select a sleeping bag according to planned use, your size and sleeping habits, and cost. Prices range from about $55 to well over $150. Here a typical selection. Above, left to right: *The Superlight*—good ratio of warmth to weight; features side zipper for attaching with another bag. *The Two Hundred*—roomier, also mates with other bags, is designed for warmth. *The Expedition*—two separate bags to be used together for maximum warmth; available in large size for those over 6' tall. Below, left to right: *The Omni* —the roomiest but not the warmest. *The Double Mummy*—room for two at lighter weight than separate bags. *The Footsack*—specialized short bag for sleeping out on ledges, snowbanks; also suitable for children.

Courtesy Sierra Designs

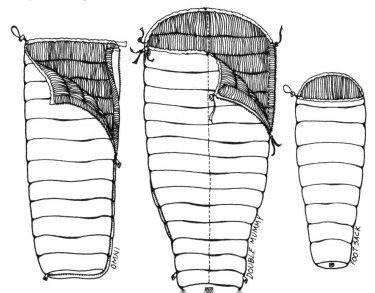

In shopping for a sleeping bag, it is generally wise to avoid the overpuffed, "top-of-the-line" bag offered by a number of manufacturers. This is sometimes described as a "winter" or "expedition" model and contains more down and elaborate construction than you would really need. If you have acquaintances who have camped out in winter, find out what types of sleeping bags they have found satisfactory. If you are setting out alone in your quest for a sleeping bag, here is a condensed shopping guide:

See what type of baffles are built into the bag to keep the down in place. Slanted wall baffles between the down segments are preferable to straight ones. The bag should be cut so that the inside diameter is smaller than the outside; what is known in the trade as differentially cut. A full-length zipper allows you more versatile use of the bag. The zipper should run down the side of the bag rather than along the center. Check the quality and type of zipper that is used. Metal zippers are apt to freeze up. Small-gauge plastic zippers are a sign of unwise economy on the part of the manufacturer.

If you find a line of three different models, the lightweight will probably be more practical than the two more elaborate and expensive types. One old-time camping trick is to put some of your clothes inside the sleeping bag with you to keep them warm and dry.

THE TRANSPORT PROBLEM

The Scandinavians have almost solved one problem—that of transporting the camping equipment. If your planned itinerary is over fairly level, rolling country, the specially designed skier's sled can be packed with necessary supplies and pulled behind you. On page 12, you can see its use as a baby carrier. The sled is attached to your waist by two fiberglass wands, which should not interfere with your skiing stride. Your main problem may be to locate one of these sleds in the United States, but a small number have been imported, and an enterprising dealer may be able to find one for you.

Most of the backpacks that are available in sizes large enough

Above, The proper wax—or climbing skins—and skillful use of the poles help in uphill treks with a heavy pack. *Below,* Packs in proportion to the size of the skiers mark a well-organized overnight camping trip.

to hold sufficient material for a winter trip have been designed for hikers rather than skiers. They ride high up on the shoulders and are free to sway, which may be ideal for hiking or even climbing, but creates problems for the skier. What you should seek is a pack that is fitted with a waist strap and designed for some inherent stability when carried. Here, you may look to European imports for the most satisfactory pack. Hikers in the United States have long been using the Bergens-type rucksack, which originated in Norway, but its use for skiers is limited, since it has a pear shape that would force you to lean too far forward in order to maintain your balance when carrying a loaded pack of this type.

The wrong type of pack can turn your expedition into a floundering, unpleasant trip through the snow. Here again, the Sierra Club comes through with the suggestion that serious skiers should try to get one of the large-style European rucksacks, the Millet from France, the Salewa from Germany, or the Karrimore from England. The pack should, of course, be waterproof and have zippered outside pockets so that you can pack supplies to be easily available without having to open the main part of the pack. It should be low and stable and not protrude too far to the rear. Ideally, about 70 percent of the weight you are carrying in the pack should be transferred to your hips and legs by the use of the waist strap.

TENTS

The old army-type pup tent which is available in so many surplus stores is hopelessly inadequate for winter camping. What you need for minimum comfort and safety is called the mountain tent, but even among these you have to do some careful shopping to get one that is really suitable. A number of companies offer do-it-yourself kits, and if you have a heavy-duty sewing machine available and some expertise in sewing, you may be able to produce satisfactory results.

Basically, the tent should be large enough to hold the desired

Mountain tents for camping under severe weather conditions.
Courtesy Gerry Division, Outdoor Sports Industries

number of persons and their gear and should be designed to *spill* the wind rather than resist it. The floor and the lower section of the tent should be of waterproof material.

The panels and ridgeline of properly made mountain tents are sewed on what is called the catenary cut, to draw tightly without wrinkling. Preferably poles should be of light aluminum and fastened both to the top and bottom of the tent. Many tents come with a cooking hole that is covered with a zippered flap as part of the door.

The two-man tent is usually about 4½ by 7 feet long and about 4 feet high. It is planned for sleeping or shelter, not for stand-up comfort. A four-man tent should be about 8 feet square, with three or four supporting poles.

The most popular tents are made of light, rip-proof nylon and

A tent suitable for three.
Courtesy Sierra Designs

The "glacier tent" for winter camping, front and rear views.
Courtesy Sierra Designs

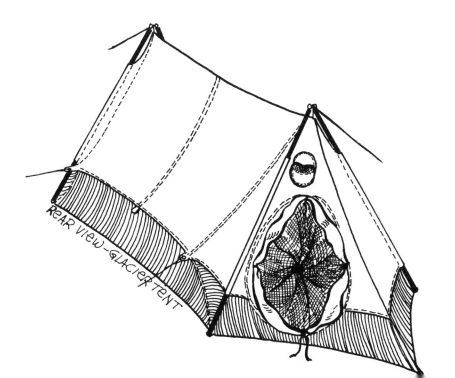

usually weigh something under 2 ounces per square yard. This fabric is windproof, yet allows some "breathing" for air transfer. One caution about tenting—one should try to avoid touching the sides of the tent, as this allows moisture to penetrate the fabric. Also, since your tent becomes part of the burden you must carry on the trail, choose as light a model as possible and avoid any frills such as frost liners or extra fly sheets. By rule of thumb, the tent should not weigh more than 3 pounds per person; a two-man tent should weigh 6 pounds or less, a four-man tent no more than 12 pounds.

As for tent pitching—that comes with a little experience. If you have the opportunity, try setting up the tent in a snow-filled area before starting out on a trip. A few points to remember: Do *not* pitch your tent under a tree, as falling snow from the branches could collapse it; keep the door side of the tent away from prevailing winds; plan ahead on just what objects you will use to hold down the corners and guy lines (some use skis and poles for this while others find that small metal disks make good snow anchors); see whether your tent is fitted with snow flaps on which you can pile snow to keep the wind from getting under the tent.

FOOD AND COOKING

You can worry about a balanced diet after you get home from a winter camping trip. Food on the trail and in camp should be as simple and substantial as possible. One-pot meals, stews, mushes, and heavy soups are the best. Plan the food with the minimum carrying weight, eliminating canned foods, for this would require transporting the liquid portions of the contents on your back. While most dehydrated foods would not win four stars from any gourmet, they are practical for trail use. Cheese, bacon, fats, and cereals provide heat energy and are lightweight.

Readily available items for snacks should be carried.

Shop around in an army surplus store for lightweight, nested cooking equipment. Keep in mind that plastic plates and utensils are more practical for cold, outdoor eating than are metal ones. In really icy weather, avoid touching cold metals with your bare hands.

As for water for drinking and cooking, while melting snow may sound adventurous, this writer has found that planning a campsite near available water is best, carrying your own water supply is second best. It takes a surprisingly large amount of powdered snow to become a potful of water, and somehow pots full of snow seem to have a way of burning through at the bottom before the snow melts.

SUGGESTIONS FOR THE BEGINNER

If you are planning a winter camping trip and have no previous outdoor living experience, these suggestions may help:

- First try a few nights of camping in summer to get the feel of it.
- Get some summer trail-camping experience. Learn to pack your rucksack; practice fire lighting, outdoor cooking, erecting the tent, and map and compass reading if you are planning an out-of-the-way trip.
- If at all possible, plan your first overnight or weekend winter camping trip to a place where a winter cabin, camp, or some other indoor sleeping facilities are available in case the weather changes for the worse or you or some other member of the group "chickens out."

WINTER CAMPING
EQUIPMENT CHECKLIST

The following checklist is a sample list that might be useful to ski tourers who plan to camp. In all likelihood, no one would ever carry all the listed items. Each person should develop his or her own checklist of equipment based on experience and needs.

Carry in Day Pack or Pack in Outer Pockets:

canteen (1 quart plastic or aluminum bottle)

At the campsite, the shovels come out and work begins on snow shelters.

Courtesy Crested Butte, Colorado

lunch for the trail

sweater and/or windbreaker if not worn

poncho

first aid kit (including moleskin, needles and thread, adhesive tape, bandaids, antiseptic, gauze, tweezers, etc.)

toilet kit (including tissues, soap, etc.)

Place in Pack:

sleeping bag

mattress (plus ¼ " closed cell foam pad)

ground cloth (plastic sheet)

tent (one or two man backpacking tent; lashing)

cooking/eating gear (including stove, two pots and frying pan, fuel bottle, extra matches in match safe, fire inspirator, gum rubber tube, light tin plate, nesting fork/spoon, small container of soap, pot scourer. Gear may include the following optional material: food soaking jar with widemouth in plastic; plastic basin, light spatula, cooking spoon, jacksaw for cutting firewood)

foodbag: 1 lb. to 1 lb. 8 oz. food per man/day is generally sufficient if menus are well planned. The weight will be much greater if no care is taken.

clothing bag (including one change of clothing, extra wool shirt or sweater, two pair extra socks, down vest or jacket for evening in camp. Moccasins or down booties for wear in camp are optional)

Common Equipment:

The following items in the list above should be shared in order to cut down individual loads:

cooking equipment

food

first aid equipment, burn preventive, soap

map, compass, guidebook

camera, binoculars (optional)

Many **schools** in the snow country have **added** winter camping ski trips to their extra-curricular activities. Here students from the Stowe School, Stowe, Vermont, are shown in their tents. The school has now switched to the use of four man tents, heating them with Coleman lanterns.

Photo by Peter Miller, courtesy John J. Handler, Jr., Headmaster Stowe School

6

SAFETY
FOR THE SKI-TOURER
AND CAMPER

The ski tourer avoids the fast downhill runs that account for so many of the accidents in Alpine skiing. In ski touring, the problems that may arise are those that accompany long exposure to cold weather. One of the more recent developments that has created some problems for ski tourers is the proliferation of snowmobiles that share the trails used by skiers in some areas.

Until you acquire some experience in ski touring, it may be best to restrict your travels to marked ski trails. On a long trip or through unfamiliar terrain provide yourself with a map and compass. If you are traveling with a group, make certain that the party remains together. It is always safest to limit the speed of the trip to that of the slowest member of the party. On camping or mountaineering trips, utilize the safety equipment described in this chapter.

Also, in difficult terrain, keep an eye open for major landmarks that will help you retrace your trail.

Another problem is winter weather, which can change almost without notice. Plan a trip so that you can turn back if conditions worsen, again keeping in mind the skiing abilities of the weakest skiers in the group.

The Sierra Club stresses that avalanches are a major threat in wilderness skiing. New snowfalls, which provide the most exciting skiing, also bring the greatest avalanche danger. The Sierra Club totebook *Wilderness Skiing* has an excellent chapter on this subject.

Adequate preparation can help to minimize the hazards of winter for the ski tourer or the winter camper.

A CAUTION FOR SKI TOURERS: THINK HYPOTHERMIA

If you are outdoors for recreation, you presumably do not intend to jeopardize your life. Hypothermia may be a new word to you, but it is the only word to describe the rapid, progressive mental and physical collapse that accompanies the chilling of the inner core of the human body. Hypothermia is caused by exposure to cold, aggravated by wet, wind, and exhaustion. It is the number one killer of outdoor recreationists.

Safety counselors advise these four basic cautions:
1. Take heed of "hypothermia weather."
2. Watch carefully for warning symptoms.
3. Choose equipment with hypothermia in mind.
4. *Think hypothermia.*

Safety Equipment

Choose rainclothes that are proof against wind-driven rain and that cover head, neck, trunk, and legs. Polyurethane-coated nylon is best. However, the coating will not last forever. Inspect the garment carefully and test under a cold shower before you leave home. Ponchos are poor protection in wind.

Take woolen clothing for hypothermia weather: two-piece woolen underwear or long wool pants and sweater or shirt. Include a knit cap that can protect neck and chin. Cotton underwear is worse than useless when wet.

A stormproof tent gives the best shelter. Take plastic sheeting and nylon twine for rigging additional foul-weather shelter.

Carry trail food—nuts, dried meats, and candy—and keep

nibbling during hypothermia weather.

Take along a gas stove or a plumber's candle, flammable paste, or some other reliable fire starter.

The Effects of Hypothermia

Cold kills in two distinct steps. The moment your body begins to lose heat faster than it produces it, you are undergoing exposure. Two things happen: Either you voluntarily exercise to stay warm, or your body makes involuntary adjustments to preserve normal temperature in the vital organs. Either response drains your energy reserves. The only way to stop the drain is to reduce the degree of exposure. *The time to prevent hypothermia is during the period of exposure and gradual exhaustion.*

If exposure continues until your energy reserves are depleted, cold reaches the brain, depriving you of judgment and reasoning power. You will not realize that this is happening, and you will lose control of your hands.

This is hypothermia. Your internal temperature is sliding downward. Without treatment, this slide leads to stupor, collapse, and death.

COLD WEATHER DEFENSES

The First Defense: Avoid Exposure

Your first line of defense is to avoid exposure. When clothes get wet, they lose about 90 percent of their insulating value. Wool loses less; cotton, down, and synthetics lose more.

Beware of the wind. A slight breeze carries heat away from the skin much faster than still air. Wind drives cold air under and through clothing, it refrigerates wet clothes by evaporating moisture from the surface, and it multiplies the problems of staying dry.

Air Temperature Need Not Be Low

Most hypothermia cases develop in air temperatures of between 30 and 50 degrees F. Most outdoorsmen simply cannot believe that these temperatures can be dangerous, and they fatally underestimate the danger of being wet at such temperatures. Fifty-degree water is unbearably cold. The cold that kills is cold water running down neck and legs, cold water held against the body by sopping clothes, cold water flushing body heat from the surface of the clothes.

The Second Defense: Terminate Exposure

If you cannot stay dry and warm under existing conditions using the clothing you have with you, terminate exposure. Have enough common sense to give up your goal, whether that of completing a tour or reaching a destination. Get out of the wind and rain. Build a fire. Concentrate on making your camp or bivouac as secure and comfortable as possible. Persistent or violent shivering is a clear warning that you are on the verge of hypothermia. Make camp while you still have a reserve of energy. Allow for the fact that exposure greatly reduces your normal endurance.

You may think that you are doing fine when the fact that you are exercising is the only thing keeping you from going into hypothermia. If exhaustion forces you to stop, however briefly, these three things may happen:

1. Your rate of body-heat production may instantly drop by 50 percent or more.
2. Violent, incapacitating shivering may begin immediately.
3. You may slip into hypothermia in a matter of minutes.

The Third Defense: Be Alert for Warning Signs

If you or your party are exposed to wind, cold, and wet, watch yourself and others for these symptoms:

1. Uncontrollable fits of shivering.
2. Vague, slow, slurred speech.
3. Memory lapses, incoherence.
4. Immobilized or fumbling hands.

5. Frequent stumbling, lurching gait.
6. Drowsiness (to sleep is to die).
7. Apparent exhaustion, inability to get up after a rest.

The Fourth Defense: Treatment

Because the onset of hypothermia is subtle and often ignored, the victim will often deny he is in trouble. Believe the symptoms, not the patient. Even mild symptoms demand immediate action.

1. Get the victim out of the wind and rain.
2. Strip off *all* clothes.
3. If the patient is only mildly impaired:
   (a.) Give him warm drinks.
   (b.) Get him into dry clothes and a warm sleeping bag. Well-wrapped warm (not hot) rocks or canteens will hasten recovery.
4. If the patient is semiconscious or worse:
   (a.) Try to keep him awake. Give warm drinks.
   (b.) Leave him stripped. Put him in a sleeping bag with another person (also stripped). If you have a double bag, put the victim between two warmth donors. Skin-to-skin contact is the most effective treatment.
5. Build a fire to warm the camp.
6. If possible, send for prompt medical aid.

Ground-to-Air Signals

If you are in a situation where you or a group might be the object of an air or ground search, you should know these signals:

BRUSH ON SNOW   TRAMPED IN SNOW   3 FIRES

SIGNALS

Viewing Area
RS-36

 Kennel
RS-45

WINTER RECREATION

 Sleeping Shelter
RS-37

 Cross-Country Skiing
RS-46

 Campground*
RS-38

 Downhill Skiing*
RS-47

 Picnic Shelter
RS-39

 Ski Jumping
RS-48

 Trailer Sites*
RS-40

 Sledding*
RS-49

 Trailer Sanitary Station
RS-41

 Ice Skating
RS-50

 Campfires*
RS-42

 Ski Bobbing*
RS-51

 Trail Shelter
RS-43

 Snowmobiling*
RS-52

 Picnic Area*
RS-44

 Winter Recreation Area
RS-77

The national parks and forests have adopted a system of standardized symbols indicating winter recreation areas and other areas, which can serve as signposts to the ski tourer. A red diagonal slash across these signs means that the activity portrayed is forbidden.

GROUND SIGNALS AID AIR SEARCHERS

Visible emergency signals are easily made in large open areas: SOS stamped in large open snowfields or grassy meadows. Pile brush in rows or put boughs in tramped snow.

Brush arrows indicating your direction of travel will aid searchers. Smoke signals in clear weather are the most effective means of attracting searchers.

Audible signals repeated at regular intervals (3 gun shots, 3 whistles or noises of any kind) will assist them in locating you. Do not signal at night, because searchers do not travel in darkness.

1. Require doctor— serious injury	2. Require medical supplies	4. Require food and water	7. Am proceeding in this direction	6. Indicate direction & proceed
13. No— negative	14. Yes— affirmative	15. Not Understood	11. All well	3. Unable to proceed

GROUND TO AIR EMERGENCY CODE
Use material which gives the maximum contrast with the background.

MAN IN THE COLD ENVIRONMENT

Man's survival anywhere in the world depends on his knowledge of life's necessities and what can harm his body, his mind, and his equipment. His ability to combat these enemies or improvise ways to provide necessities may be his greatest challenge.

If the skier is to be able to survive anywhere his feet can carry him, he should have knowledge of all aspects of the terrain and weather under all conditions, with all the stresses that could or might prevail. Of course, it would require volumes to cover all the variables of survival, but the primary concern to the ski tourer, camper, or ski mountaineer is the effect of cold and wet on the body.

The first factor to consider is the psychological one, for the mind controls all physical movement, as well as judgment. Loss of mental control may allow man's determination to drive him on and on to exhaustion of his limited available energy.

Excessive cold has a detrimental effect on the mind and even on muscle movement and can upset the delicate heat balance required within the body, so it is important to learn how to stay warm for survival in the cold.

Physical requirements for survival in cold and wet climates are basically simple. And if one is aware of the consequences of being without them, he may be able to improvise protection from what surrounds him, such as providing protective shelter for the body.

Cold and the Primary Physiological Responses

Cold affects not just one or two specific tissues or functions of the exposed person; but the whole physiological economy in sometimes subtle, yet always complex fashion.

Under cold conditions, humidity plays a minor role unless the skin is artificially wetted by rain or perspiration. Should this occur, the resultant evaporation cooling may exceed all other factors in importance. A man immersed in sub-arctic, 40-degree water can be cooled beyond recovery in about twenty to forty minutes, or in approximately ten to twenty minutes in 32-degree water. A man in wet cotton clothing must consider himself nearly immersed in water and must act accordingly.

The interactive effects of air temperature and air movement are so inseparable under cold conditions that the term "wind chill" is widely used to designate their combined effects.

The regulatory process called into play to maintain the 99-degree heat balance in a cold environment represents a primary burden on the body, and in turn sets up disturbances that increase the total burden on the body.

The first regulatory action to be initiated when the body cools is constriction of the blood vessels of the skin, reducing the blood flow and lowering the skin temperature so that heat loss by conduction and radiation is decreased. Muscle tone is enhanced, and the desire for voluntary exercise is experienced. With further cooling of the blood the automatic, involuntary shivering reaction occurs. This increases the heat production to eightfold for a short time, but such expenditure of energy quickly fatigues the body and often occurs as the body's last-ditch effort to stay warm before succumbing to hypothermia. Other physiological reactions such as increased appetite and blood pressure changes occur during blood cooling, but are of secondary consequence. Frostbite often occurs because the sensory nerve endings become less excitable with the constriction of blood vessels. Therefore, a man often fails to recognize the danger in time to prevent freezing of the flesh.

How Body Heat Is Lost

Man feels the "cold" when body heat is being exchanged between him and his environment by any of these five physical processes: evaporation, conduction, convection, radiation, and respiration. Heat will be exchanged by conduction between the surface of the body and any material in contact with it which is at a different temperature. The speed of transfer is basically determined by the difference in temperature of the two and by the heat-conducting properties of the material. If the contacting substance is fluid, such as air or water, continuous movement of the fluid accelerates the transfer of heat. This process is called convection. Nearly all transfer of "sensible" heat between the skin and air around the body is by the combined process of conduction and convection.

Heat may be lost from the body surface to the air by evaporation of water diffusing through the skin through perspiration or when water is applied—or accidentally applied—to the body surface, in rain or by immersion or wet clothing. The rate of heat loss is determined by the difference in temperature and the movement of air and the amount of water or saturation of the

111

clothing. This process is called evaporation.

When we feel something "cold," the body is giving up its heat to something. We can reduce this rate of heat exchange by adding clothing, by substituting some insulating material between the skin and that which has a lower temperature, or by acquiring shelter that encloses the air of 75 degrees F. temperature with no air movement.

Effect of Clothing in Cold Environments

Clothing is only a protective shelter that we carry around. The immediate effect of adding clothing to the nude body is to trap a certain thickness of virtually dead, body-warmed air from the cooler air that was formerly circulating past the body. The effectiveness of the clothing will depend on the rate at which heat passes across the space between the skin and clothing and through the clothing barrier.

Transfer across the space between skin and clothing depends on the distance between them and on the rate of air movement within the space. Where clothing touches the skin, as when clothing is pressed against the body by contact with the colder ground or solid objects, by wind or by the hang of the clothing, the transfer of heat will be rapid. And where wet clothing touches the skin, the resultant conduction and evaporation heat loss will be rapid—often at the same rate as immersion heat loss.

Transfer of heat through clothing may take place in several ways: by conduction through the fibers, such as metallic fibers in the clothing, nails in shoes, buttons, etc.; through conduction, convection, radiation, evaporation; or through the dead air held in the interstices between the fibers of the weave. If water replaces a large part of the interstices, then the heat conductivity of the fabric is greatly increased. Such wetness greatly increases heat loss by evaporation and conduction. This can become the outdoorsman's greatest problem in stormy weather.

The radiation-absorption effect of clothing can be a great help in cold environments. Dark clothing absorbs radiant heat from

112

the sun, and reflective clothing repels heat. The openings of clothing—neck, arm and leg cuffs, and zipper openings—all contribute to heat loss to some degree and often allow the greatest amount of heat loss owing to the pumping action of warm air next to the skin during body movement.

Cold that affects the body can be minor or severe. The backyard wind that chills the skin and numbs the fingers is just a reminder that the body surfaces need better protection or a change of environment. The cold felt by a person out in a wet, windy snowstorm can set up physiological reactions in the body that can be fatal in a few hours without adequate body protection.

The type of fabric and the cut of the clothing have much to do with its insulation value, freedom of movement, constriction of blood flow, warm-air transfer, water retention, and ventilation of excess body heat generated by muscle action during outdoor exercise.

To the outdoorsman, dependent on the clothes he wears and carries to keep his body warm, dry, and sheltered during his travels, the choice of clothing should have the highest priority. Because of weight limitations, weather factors, seasonal conditions, and the environment, his clothing must serve many purposes, yet be strong enough to withstand the abuse of the rough, rugged environment.

Cold-Weather Clothing

Several layers of easy-on, easy-off, lightweight clothing offer layers of dead air for insulation between the fabrics. Wool is preferable, as it is a nonabsorbing fabric and has the unique property of keeping the body warm even when the fabric is wet. However, the loose weave of the woolen fabric leaves much to be desired in a windstorm. So a wind stopper is advisable as an outer garment to minimize loss of the body-warmed air trapped in the large air sacs of the weave.

Cotton fabric has excellent properties in warm or moderate climates and even provides an excellent layer system of dead-air spaces which give insulation against cold, as long as the cloth remains dry. The danger of cotton is that it absorbs and retains water, making it a deadly combination when it gets wet from rain, snow, or perspiration. Cotton is very slow to dry because of the complete saturation of the fibers. Cotton clothing can become so saturated with water that the body-heat loss can be nearly as great as when the body is totally immersed in water. Very wet cotton can lose heat nearly 240 times faster than dry cotton clothing.

To the man who continually produces excess heat by nearly constant burning of energy to move muscles, perspiration wetness is a perplexing problem that requires alert and constant attention to ventilation. The outdoorsman often has to slow his pace considerably just to prevent wetness of underclothes. In extreme cold, windy conditions, he must quickly substitute dry clothing or find warm shelter once he stops exercising, or he will experience chilling and excessive body-heat loss.

Minimize sweating. It is dangerous because it leads to freezing. When exerting yourself, cut down sweating by opening your clothes at the neck and wrists and loosening the waist. If you are still warm, remove mittens and headgear, or take off a layer or two of outer clothing. When you stop work, put your clothes on again to prevent chilling.

Wear clothing loosely. Tight-fitting clothes cut off circulation and increase the danger of freezing. Keep your head and ears covered. Don't allow your boots to become too tight by wearing too many socks. Keep clothes as clean as possible. Replace buttons and repair holes promptly. In strong wind or extreme cold, wrap yourself in plastic or paper, or get into your shelter.

At night, arrange dry spare clothing loosely around your shoulders and kidney area. When you are cold, breathe through a loose-weave cloth or a face mask. Breath moisture will freeze in below-freezing temperatures and seal a tight-fitting mask, so be sure the scarf, sweater, or mask is always loose. Cold air is warmed by the body to approximately 98

114

degrees, at the expense of energy. Prolonged exposure is harmful to lung tissues.

If you fall into water in a cold environment, hasten into dry clothing. If this is not possible, roll in dry snow to blot up moisture. Roll, then brush off the snow; roll again and again until all water has been absorbed by the snow. Do not take off your shoes until you are in shelter. Change to dry clothing as soon as possible. The cold will be intense once you are wet, and in a few minutes you will be incapable of removing your clothing without a buddy's assistance. Never travel alone.

In very low temperatures, wet clothing can be dried by freezing, then beating the ice crystals out of the fabric.

Prevention of getting wet is far better than clever techniques of redrying. Avoid all open water. Don't cross a snow-covered lake unless you are sure there is firm ice, sufficient to support your weight, under the snow. Stay dry—it is the way to stay alive in the cold.

SHELTER

Shelter is only clothing at a distance. It may or may not include artificial heat producers such as stoves. A shelter may be constructed of any material—lumber, bark, paper, cardboard, plastic, snow, or dirt—and may utilize insulation materials—snow, dirt, paper, fabric, bark, wood, cardboard, air—to help reduce body-heat loss by convection, evaporation, radiation, or conduction.

In emergency situations such as windstorms and rainstorms, where shelter is mandatory, man would be wise to do what the local animals do—burrow in, or crawl under foliage. In forested areas it is faster to burrow or to hollow out a small shelter under a downed tree than to find suitable material to erect a shelter. Time spent constructing such a shelter can be costly in energy and body-heat loss owing to more exposure to the very conditions one is seeking shelter from. Firelight and warmth are a comfort, but not if you must be further exposed to hostile elements. Attempting to build a fire in rain may be

115

futile—not only is it nearly impossible, but you just get wetter gathering fuel. Seek shelter and stay dry.

A shelter must serve the immediate needs of the builder. Each shelter should be built to provide a minimum of body-heat loss and a maximum of body protection.

Basic Survival Shelters

CLOSED SHELTERS

Closed or small-area shelters sealed against the wind, rain, and cold are necessary in cold environments where body heat is used as the primary heat source. These shelters can provide a minimum of cold-air transfer with the outside cold air. All closed types of shelters should be small and have all holes plugged with snow, bark, dirt, or boughs, unless a gas stove or open flame is used in the shelter, which would require a high and low vent to remove carbon monoxide.

In a forested area, burrow in under a log; use bark and boughs as siding material and ground insulation. This is by far the quickest and least energy-consuming technique.

In areas devoid of forest, dig snow caves or snow trenches, or build rockeries to gain the desired protection. Snow caves take hours to build and require some type of tool, such as a shovel, mess kit, or hard hat, for removing the snow. Snow is a good insulator. Caves dug into deep snowbanks are quite satisfactory. Keep your clothing dry when digging. Work slowly to avoid excessive sweating. Perspiration-wet underclothes should be changed or removed and used as outer clothing once they are wet.

A snow cave in deep powder snow necessitates special construction and requires about three hours to complete. First select two 6-foot sticks. Drive one vertically into the ground, and use the other to draw a 12-foot circle around this stake. When finished, place the stick on the ground with one end touching the stake. Shovel the fluffy snow into the circle, packing it down until it is approximately 1 foot above the vertical

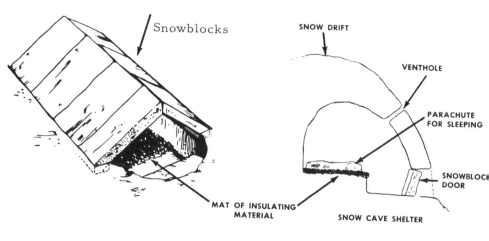

Snowblocks

MAT OF INSULATING MATERIAL

SNOW DRIFT

VENTHOLE

PARACHUTE FOR SLEEPING

SNOWBLOCK DOOR

SNOW CAVE SHELTER

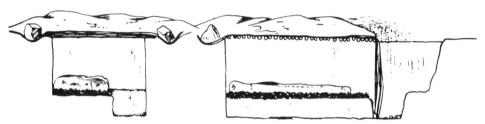

SNOW TRENCH

Basic Survival Shelters.

Powder-snow cave.

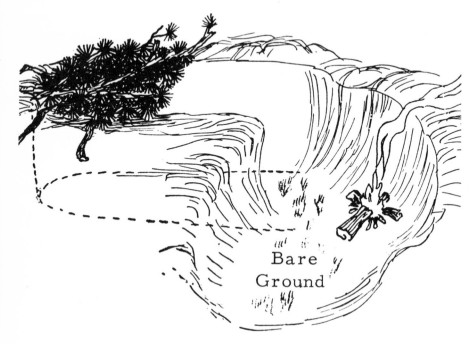

Bare
Ground

Powder-snow pit shelter.

stake. Let the snowpile set for about an hour; then tunnel into the pile, following the guide stick. Remove snow to the warmer ground, and make a small room with 2-foot-thick walls. Remove vertical stake.

OPEN-SIDE SHELTER

In forested areas, where you have an ample supply of boughs, bark, and limbs, a simple bough-roofed shelter will give some protection from rain, wind, and snow. Construction takes time and energy and offers only a minimum of body protection. A fire and a heat reflector can help dry clothing.

Tree pit shelter.
Drawings courtesy Tacoma Mountain Rescue Unit

UNDER-THE-LOG SHELTER

Mountain rescue personnel advocate the simple under-the-log shelter. Find a log with a hole under it. Hollow it out. Use slabs of bark to enclose your nest. Plug all holes. Keep living area small.

TREE-PIT SHELTER

In wooded country make a tree-pit shelter if the snow is deep enough. Enlarge the natural pit around a large tree trunk, and roof it with any readily available covering—ice blocks, branches, or canvas. Use boughs and bark for insulation.

Camp in timber, if possible, to be near fuel. If you can't find timber, choose any spot protected from wind and drifting snow. Don't camp at the base of slopes or cliffs where snow may drift or come down in avalanches.

119

Try to keep the openings of all shelters cross wind, and construct a windbreak.

HAZARDS OF COLD ENVIRONMENTS

Cold is miserable unless you have planned and prepared for it, with adequate body protection. The effect of cold on an unmittened hand is numbness of fingers.

Frostbite: Should you accidentally incur frostbite, you will recognize it by the grayish or yellow-white spots on the skin. Warm the frozen part rapidly on the bare flesh under the armpits or stomach. If hot water is available for the thawing procedure, use nothing hotter than 105 degrees. Do not rub frozen flesh or forcibly remove gloves or shoes. Once frozen flesh is thawed, do not allow it to refreeze.

Freezing: You will freeze only if the air is carrying away more heat than your body can generate. If you prevent the cold air from reaching your skin, by wearing proper clothing or shelter and keeping your body heat in balance, you won't freeze.

You can sleep or doze safely in cold areas with little danger of freezing, provided you are in good physical condition and have ample energy reserve. Your brain will awaken you when the body cools to the point at which it needs exercise to create body heat. Exercise arms, legs, and trunk to increase circulation and generate body heat. Then it is safe to doze again. Do not attempt this without a good reserve of energy.

Snow blindness: This is caused by exposure of the unprotected eye to the glare on snow. This can occur even on cloudy days. Prevention is the best cure. Wear dark glasses, or improvise glare shades by cutting small slits in any material suitable to tie around the head. Treatment of snow blindness is with cold compresses and aspirin and by wearing a lightproof bandage. The victim will generally recover in eighteen to twenty hours but must use caution to prevent recurrence.

Sunburn: Sunburn can occur in snow country. Cover up in

bright sunlight. Use approved sun creams. Reflected sunlight can burn inside the nostrils, under the chin, and in the ears. Don't compound an emergency with more problems—cover up and prevent sunburn.

Carbon Monoxide Poisoning: This is a great danger in cold areas where gasoline stoves must be used to prepare meals and for light. This poisonous gas is colorless and odorless. Prevention is easy—maintain good ventilation when a fire is burning. Never fall asleep without turning out the stove or lamp. Never leave one burning unattended.

Carbon monoxide burns in a blue flame but is freely generated by a yellow flame. If you see a yellow flame, check your ventilation quickly. Check stoves under pots often. If the fire burns blue with the pot off, the stove is operating correctly.

Usually there are no symptoms of carbon monoxide poisoning. Unconsciousness and death may occur without previous warning. Sometimes victims may feel pressure at the temples, burning eyes, headache, and pounding pulse. Treat by getting into fresh air and, if necessary, applying artificial respiration.

Dehydration: This is almost as great a problem in cold conditions as on the desert, because all the water is frozen into snow or ice. Some streams or lakes may provide access to water (use extreme caution against falling into the water). If the sun is shining, you can melt snow on a dark plastic, a tarp, a flat rock, or any surface that will absorb the sun's heat. If you melt snow by heating it over a stove or fire, put in a little snow at a time and compress it—or the pot will burn. Agitating, as with a stick or knife, will speed up the melting time. If water is available, put a little in the bottom of the pot and add snow gradually. If ice is available, use it. You get more water for the volume with less heat and time.

If fuel is plentiful, try to drink at least two quarts of hot beverages or water daily, instead of cold water. Water taken internally will be heated to 99 degrees at the expense of energy loss.

Travel in Cold Environments

If the decision to travel has been reached, after consideration of the requirements of food, fuel, shelter, and destination, equip yourself as best you can. Don't travel in whiteouts, blizzards, or bitter-cold winds. Make camp and save your strength until better weather. Never travel with poor visibility. Use available equipment or improvise equipment to meet your needs. Carry or sled all your clothing, sleeping bags, food, and fuel.

STAYING ALIVE IN A COLD EMERGENCY
First Stage

Get out of rain—wind—storm.

Make body shelter. Improvise quickest adequate type for terrain and conditions.

Analyze the approximate length of the emergency and chances of assistance.

Analyze personal dangers:
>Severity of body-heat loss.
>Local environmental hazards.
>Amount of remaining energy.

Analyze resources:
>Adequate clothing—insulation.
>Emergency equipment—shelter—warmth—fire—signals.
>Transportation.

Add body insulation—loose-fitting wool clothing in layers.
>Shelter the head and neck from wind and cold.
>Close all clothing openings.

Put on windproof and rainproof clothing to reduce heat loss.

Improvise artificial heat—fire—stoves, etc.

Stay put in shelter until conditions improve. Conserve energy.

Do not travel if visibility is obscured.

Second Stage

Don't get wet. Wet clothing loses body heat 240 times faster than dry clothing.

Don't sweat. Indicates excessive energy loss and gets clothing wet from inside.

Stay calm. Worry causes imagination to blossom; imagination causes poor judgment.

Conserve energy. Don't travel in a storm.

The remaining energy is all you have to produce lifesaving body heat.

Stay comfortable. Add clothing insulation as needed.

Loose-fitting clothing in layers creates a dead-air-space insulation.

Shelter head and neck. Close all clothing openings.

Put on windproof and rainproof clothing to minimize wetness and body-heat loss.

Nibble food and drink.

Get artificial heat—fire, if possible. Drink hot drinks.

Nibble on food to resupply energy.

If food is not available, conserve what energy you have.

Stay put. Don't fight a storm.

If visibility is obscured, don't travel. Shelter is the primary need.

Most storms are of short duration.

Tips:

Prewarm inhaled air by breathing through a wool cloth or scarf.

Sit and stand on thick insulation.

Keep stored water from freezing.

Stay dry. Don't sweat.

If skin is numb, watch for frostbite.

When traveling or working, watch for signs of stumbling, poor reflexes, careless attitude. They indicate exhaustion—and exhaustion can be thirty minutes from death.

Watch for equipment damage by cold. Protect fuel and water supply.

Improvise mittens, overboots, and body insulation.

Pioneers have survived severe storms by wearing bark from trees.

The following material and literature is available from the nonprofit Mountain Rescue Council, Tacoma Unit. PO Box 696, Tacoma, Washington 98401:

Simple Basic-Preparedness Kits

Storm Kit—11 oz.	$2.00
Storm Shelter—5 oz.	$1.00

Basic Information Books and Brochures

Outdoor Living	$2.50
(teachers, leaders)	
Mountaineering Medicine	$1.00
(all outdoorsmen)	
Careless Ev Cartoons	$1.00
(ten 8½ by 11-inch cartoons and one plastic frame)	
Survival Lecture Outlines	$ .50

Outdoor Safety Literature

These awareness brochures are free on individual request. Donation of mailing charges would be appreciated.

Hiking and Backpacking Safety
Back Country Safety (hunters)
Fatigue–Exhaustion–Energy
Street Signs of the Wilderness
Survival—Arctic to Desert

PART IV

Cross-Country Competition

Public relations firms have been quick to climb on the bandwagon as
ski touring and cross-country racing become more and more popular.
Here, a commercially sponsored race at Yosemite gets underway.
Courtesy of the Christian Brothers of California

7

NORDIC CROSS-COUNTRY COMPETITION: RECREATIONAL AND ATHLETIC

There is something about getting on a pair of skis that seems to spur the competitive spirit. As soon as a person is able to push himself along over the snow without falling, he begins to wonder whether he can do it faster than someone else.

For the recreational skier there are the USSA (United States Ski Association) medals for mileage covered on skis during a winter skiing season, or whatever constitutes a "season" in his locale.

The NASTAR (National Standard Race) is a commercially sponsored program that allows the skier to earn a handicap rating, somewhat similar to a handicap in golf.

In the more formalized Nordic competitions under regulations of the FIS (Fédération Internationale de Ski) and in Olympic competition, there are medals offered in twelve events, far more than in the Alpine events.

Male competitors run 15-, 30-, and 50-kilometer races. The last is considered one of the most grueling physical competitions in the sports world. In addition, there is a four-man relay in which each competitor skis 10 kilometers. Women competitors ski over 5- and 10-kilometer courses, with each member of a three-woman relay team doing 5 kilometers. Ski jumping is also considered one of the Nordic events, with competition on the "small" hill of 70 meters and the "big" hill of over 90 meters. The Nordic Combined Competition requires both cross-country ski performance and jumping.

The Biathlon events combine cross-country racing with rifleshooting, with penalty minutes subtracted from the entrant's score for missed targets. There are both individual and team Biathlon events.

As yet, the United States skiers have had little success in international or Olympic Nordic skiing.

UNITED STATES SKI ASSOCIATION DISTANCE MEDALS

In cooperation with the President's Council on Physical Fitness & Sports, the United States Ski Association (USSA) offers recreational ski tourers an opportunity to receive medals for mileage they cover on skis during a winter ski season. Skiers are required to submit a log showing the distances they cover. The mileage required for each medal is:

Bronze	75
Silver	150
Gold	300

Only one medal is awarded against each log. If the participant retains the log to ski additional mileage for a higher award, only the highest medal will be awarded. A participant can send in the log for the lower award and then start again with a new log to try to achieve one of the higher awards.

The mileage is logged after each day's skiing by the participant. Any terrain or location may be used in attaining these medals. On measured terrain use the linear map distance plus 10 percent for terrain adjustment. Help in completing the log is available at any outlet—many ski-equipment shops or ski areas—where the Distance Medal Events placard is displayed.

USSA membership is not required to participate in Distance Medal Events, but when the mileage has been achieved, membership in the United States Ski Association (fee $7) is required for award of the medal.

When completed, the log should be mailed to:

Distance Medal Events
United States Ski Association
1726 Champa, Suite 300
Denver, Colorado 80202

Logs and rules for the President's Council award may be obtained from the USSA national office or:

The President's Council on Physical Fitness & Sports
Washington, D.C. 20202

THE NASTAR PROGRAM

The NASTAR program is described as "The National Standard Race . . . A *Ski Magazine* Program for the Recreational Skier." Sponsored by the makers of Johnnie Walker beverages, the program operates this way:

The skiers race a mild course of 2.5 kilometers. They then receive a handicap score, similar to the par system in golf. This handicap is a national standard and enables the skier to compare himself against others all over the country.

Information and application forms are available from NASTAR, PO Box 4580, Aspen, Colorado 81611. Phone 303-925-7864.

A large number of ski-touring clubs and many ski resort areas are participating in the NASTAR program. Some have weekly races during the snow season. Information on coming events in the NASTAR program will be found in the monthly *Ski Magazine* and in bulletins of the skiing clubs.

Everyone can compete in NASTAR races: *Clockwise from top left:* Mrs. Carmany Heilman of Chappaqua, New York, shows the power of concentration; C. T. Schandelmeier, sixty-six-year-old NASTAR racer and bronze medal winner from Bensenville, Illinois; Jack Armstrong of Plymouth, New Hampshire, winning his gold pin in one of the many races held at Waterville Valley, New Hampshire; another Waterville Valley NASTAR racer demonstrates the newest form of "parallel skiing"—not guaranteed to win many races.

Photos: Harry G. Curran

Photos: Scott Nelson

Never too young to begin NASTAR racing, five-year-old Rick Busch competes in his first race at Alpine Meadows, California.
Photo: Chapman Wentworth

THE BIATHLON

The Biathlon, which combines cross-country skiing with riflery, is a relatively new event in world competitions, including the Olympic Games. Its antecedents go back to the introduction of firearms in the Scandinavian countries, where matches would be held to find out who could be the most productive hunter on skis, and competition consisted of going out on skis for a certain determined time, hunting game, and returning with it to the starting point.

Later, about one hundred years ago, targets were substituted for animals, and regular courses for skiing were laid out. Competitors could test their abilities under the same conditions and so determine the best marksman and fastest skier. Since then, the Biathlon has not changed much.

In the modern Biathlon, skiers leave the starting line at thirty-second intervals, rifles strapped to their backs. They ski for several kilometers, depending on the length of the race, then flop down into a prone shooting position and take aim on a 5-inch black circle about 150 yards away. Then, as quickly as possible, the rifle is strapped back on, ski poles are snatched up, and the marksman once again becomes a skier.

On a 20-kilometer (12-mile) race, there are four major ski legs and four shooting periods. Twice the rifles are shot from a prone position and twice while standing. Twenty shots are fired, and every time the contestant misses, a minute or two is deducted from his total time, depending on how far off-center the bullet has hit.

In the Biathlon Relay Race four men race 10 kilometers each, firing at breakable targets. The marksman has three chances to hit the target and faces a short penalty lap for each shot missed. The extra factor of difficulty in the relay is that the skier is traveling faster, because of the shorter distance. The increased heartbeat under this condition makes aiming the rifle increasingly difficult.

133

Sven Johanson, who has coached the U.S. Biathlon Team for more than ten years. He also races in marathon events and offers lessons to military families.

U.S. Army Photo

The American Biathlon Team

The American Biathlon Team is basically a military operation, with training centered in the Department of the Army's U.S. Modern Winter Biathlon Training Center, northeast of Anchorage, Alaska.

The team is open to both military and civilian applicants. As the Army explains, "The training of a Biathlete calls for a man willing to devote himself completely to the sport. Prerequisites generally require either a competitive skiing background or a strong athletic background. An application should include a very thorough résumé of athletic background to include competitive results, if available.

"You may train at the center either as a civilian or service member. Basically, civilians must support themselves as we support them only to the extent of providing equipment, with lodging and meals at cost. Civilians must bear their own travel and living costs to competitions and clinics. Qualified military personnel who are accepted for training at the center are fully supported to include travel expenses to competitions."

Detailed information may be obtained by writing to:

Department of the Army
U.S. Modern Winter Biathlon Training Center
APO Seattle 98749

THE BIATHLON RULES

I. Individual Biathlon Race

COURSE

1. The Biathlon race takes place over 20 kilometers of natural country and includes four bouts of firing on the range. The course should comply with FIS and UIPM rules as nearly as local conditions and resources permit. In particular, every effort should be made to avoid the following: traverses (other than very short ones) where the racer has to ski with one foot higher than the other; a hard climb immediately before the

Biathlon team coach, Major Jack Ferguson watches a biathlete fire his Remington.
U.S. Army Photo

Elapsed time, recorded by a timer, tells whether the physical training and preparation of his skis has paid off in speed for this racer.
U.S. Army Photo

range; dangerous rocks or trees close to the fast downhill stretches and sharp turns at the bottom; deep holes or ruts across the track that may break skis; and excessively hard first 2 kilometers.

2. The course is to be marked clearly so that no competitor is left in doubt where the track goes. The marking should be colored flags or strips of paper or cloth, only one color being used throughout. In addition, every fifth kilometer and each of the last 5 kilometers should be marked by kilometer boards.

3. At suitable places on the course, controls are to be established, where the passing of each competitor is to be recorded by the controller. Each controller should have at least one assistant. A control should also be placed anywhere there is reasonable doubt where the track goes, *e.g.*, at points where part of the track is run twice, to ensure that competitors follow the right route.

4. The chief of the course must ensure that the course is prepared in good time before the race and that competitors are given ample opportunity to inspect it. On the morning of the race, the whole course must be run over by a "tracking patrol," forty-five minutes ahead of the first competitor, regardless of snow conditions. If there is further snowfall, larger reserves of forerunners will be put through the course.

5. At least forty-eight hours prior to the start, competitors must be shown or have access to a sketch map and a profile of the course on which the rifle ranges, control posts, refreshment points, and the first-aid station are indicated.

RANGE AND TARGETS

6. The range is to be 150 meters, and the firing positions are to be prone, standing, prone, standing, in that order. The shooting can take place at one or more locations. The four bouts of shooting, each of five rounds, are to take place between 4 and 18 kilometers, with at least 3 kilometers' running distance between each bout.

7. Firing points should be even and hard; the forward sec-

tion (80 centimeters and 1 meter wide) level with the line of the target, the rear section (2 to 3 meters wide) sloping backward at about 7 degrees from the forward section. The targets should not be more than 6 degrees above or below the firing point. Each competitor should have sufficient room (2.5 to 3 meters) to shoot with his skis on. Wind flags, 10 by 40 centimeters in size, of a contrasting color (not red) are to be positioned suitably on the flanks as a guide to competitors. Special shelters (*i.e.*, roofs) are not to be used on the firing line.

8. The targets are to have scoring black circular disks as follows:

Prone Position: Diameter 25 centimeters with a 12.5-centimeter diameter inner ring.

Standing Position: Diameter 50 centimeters with a 35-centimeter diameter inner ring.

They must be tacked firmly onto posts, 2 by 2 inches. No tacks should be on the black scoring disks, which should have a white border, minimum 5 centimeters wide.

EQUIPMENT

9. Choice of skis and sticks is optional.

10. Dress is optional. Clothing may be strengthened with soft leather, rubber, sheepskin, or similar material on both elbows and on the firing shoulder. It is also permissible to reduce pressure of the straps on the forward arm by using soft padding, sheepskin, or similar material on the back of the arm from the shoulder to a point 8 to 10 centimeters below the elbow in the prone position. The padding must be no more than 15 to 18 centimeters wide and must be fixed to the outside of the arm. Maximum thickness (including the cloth of the sleeve) when lightly compressed must not be more than 10 millimeters. If a glove is used on the forward hand, it must not reach more than 5 centimeters above the hand. A hook or similar device may be used on the upper part of the forward arm to prevent the strap from slipping.

11. The choice of the rifle is optional, but it must not be

Hardly a graceful athletic gesture, but this is the approved "flop" position for the prone rifle-shooting part of the Biathlon competition.
U.S. Army Photo

automatic, must have a trigger pressure of at least 1 kilogram (2.2 pounds), and be of a caliber of 8 millimeters or less. The distance between the middle of the barrel and the lower edge of the forestock must not be more than 90 millimeters. Binoculars and telescopic sights are forbidden.

12. At least twenty rounds of ammunition are to be carried; reserve ammunition may be carried. Lead bullets are not to be used.

13. When skiing, a competitor may use as many straps as he likes to carry his rifle, but only one strap may be used during shooting.

14. Waxes, reserve ski tips, reserve ammunition, and rifle spare parts may be carried.

SHOOTING POSITIONS

15. A competitor may shoot with his skis on or off as he wishes. Sticks may not be used as supports. When the competi-

tor is firing in the prone position, the forward arm may be supported by a strap not more than 40 millimeters wide and fixed to the rifle in front of the forward hand. The strap must pass around one side of the wrist and around the upper arm. A second strap or hand support is not allowed. The inside of the wrist of the forward arm must be at least 15 centimeters above the ground. The other arm must be clearly off the ground from a point 10 centimeters below the elbow joint.

16. When the competitor is firing in the standing position, the upper part and the elbow of the forward arm may be supported against the chest and hip. No support for the rifle may be used. Ammunition pouches (or the equivalent) may not be used to support the forward arm.

COURSE PROCEDURES

17. It is a competitor's own responsibility to have his skis and rifle marked officially before starting. Marked equipment is to be checked at the start and finish.

18. All competitors must wear the official numbers.

19. Competitors must follow the marked track and pass through all the control points.

20. The start is to be at one-minute intervals. The order of starting is to be decided by drawing lots in accordance with FIS rules.

21. The starter is to give every competitor a ten-second warning, followed by "Get ready—five, four, three, two, one, GO!" At the word "go," a competitor's forward foot must not be in front of the line of the gate. If, in the opinion of the starter, a competitor makes an unfair start, the starter is to recall him immediately, whereupon the competitor must return and start again, keeping his original starting time. If he fails to return, the starter must disqualify him.

22. A competitor who is not at the start at the time appointed on the official start list is to be disqualified unless the starter decides that his arrival was delayed by circumstances outside his control. In such a case, the starter will permit a

competitor to start either in a subsequent gap or at the end or at a half-minute interval at his (the starter's) discretion. The starting time of the other competitors is in no case to be altered.

23. Assistants, team captains, or reserves will not be allowed to accompany competitors on the course during the competition.

24. A competitor may exchange skis or sticks during the race, but he must finish on at least one ski marked at the start and with the same rifle.

25. At the first call of "track," the competitor who is addressed must give way by stepping out of the track if he is not in a position to outdistance his rival. The latter must not be hindered in any way from passing. A competitor who does not give way at a call of "track" will be disqualified.

26. If a competitor retires, he must announce this to the next control post or at the finish.

27. A competitor may be given wax and the means of applying it, food, drink, and information during the race (except on the firing point), but he must not be otherwise helped. No pacemaker may ski ahead, behind, or beside the competitor.

28. A competitor finishes when his first foot crosses the finish line.

29. After crossing the finish line, the competitor should proceed to have his equipment inspected.

30. As soon as possible after the race, a notice is to be posted at the race office giving the names of those disqualified, with brief reasons, or stating "No disqualifications." An individual may be disqualified if he commits an infraction of the rules.

Range Procedures

31. A competitor is to shoot all four stages. On arrival at the firing point, he is to go to the firing position indicated by the firing point officer. He is to load his rifle and fire five shots in his own time.

Lieutenant Lyle Nelson prepares to shoot after skiing four kilometers in pursuit of John Morton, already in prone firing position.

32. At the range(s), only officials in charge may come into contact with the competitor. Binoculars may be used only by officials; no spotting or outside advice whatsoever (which will lead to automatic disqualification) is allowed on the firing point, which should be roped off, and the spectators are to be kept at least 25 meters away.

33. The firing point officer is to count the five shots and check that the competitor is firing at his correct target. Misfires are to be reshot from reserve ammunition carried by the competitor. The dud cartridges are to be handed over to the firing point officer, who is to report the occurrence to the race jury immediately after the race.

34. After firing, the competitor is to unload his rifle and obtain clearance from the firing point officer before leaving the firing point. No rounds are to be left in the rifle.

35. For hits in the inner circle (prone 12.5 centimeters and standing 35 centimeters), no penalties. For a hit in the outer circle (prone 25 centimeters and standing 50 centimeters), one-minute penalty. For hits outside the scoring rings and complete misses on the target, two-minute penalty.

36. Total elapsed time from start to finish (to include range time) is the running time. Running time plus penalty minutes equals the total time for the course.

37. In the event of a tie, the competitor with the best racing time is the winner. If the racing times are equal, the competitor with the best result at the last shoot (if tie is not broken, highest score by shooting stages in inverse order) is the winner.

38. All targets are to be checked for accuracy of marking by the race jury after the race and before the official results are published. A gauge equal to the caliber of the largest-caliber rifle used by any competitor in the race is to be used to decide whether or not doubtful shots are hits or misses. Shots on a competition target which were obviously fired by another competitor (*e.g.*, wrong caliber) are to be subtracted from his results.

II. The Biathlon Relay Race

COURSE

39. The 4 × 7.5 relay race is to be run over 7.5 kilometers of natural country. The course should comply with FIS and UIPM rules as nearly as local conditions and resources permit. In particular, every effort should be made to avoid the following: traverses (other than very short ones) where the racer has to ski with one foot higher than the other; a hard climb immediately before the range; dangerous rocks or trees close to the fast downhill stretches and sharp turns at the bottom; deep holes or ruts across the track that may break skis, and excessively hard first 2 kilometers.

40. Apart from a different start, and possibly a different finish, the same 7.5-kilometer course is to be used for each lap of the race.

41. The course is to be marked clearly so that no competitor is left in doubt where the track goes.

42. The start, relay zone, and finish are all to be on level ground. The run-in to the finish and to the relay zone is to consist of a double track for at least 100 and preferably 500 meters.

43. Rules 3 and 4 also apply to the Biathlon relay.

44. Each competitor is to have his own individual track from the start for at least 100 meters. Thereafter, the starting tracks are to converge gradually into the common tracks for a distance of at least another 100 meters.

45. The start line is to be drawn in a slight circle so that teams have the same distance to cover before reaching the common track.

46. A penalty loop of 200 meters will be prepared just past the range off the main course.

RANGE AND TARGETS

47. The two stages of shooting are to take place at approximately the 2.5-kilometer (prone) and 5-kilometer (standing) marks. The range is 150 meters. Rule 7 also applies to the relay race.

48. Targets will be of a breakable material that will clearly indicate a hit to the competitor.

49. The diameter of the destructible targets will be 12.5 centimeters (for the prone position) and 30 centimeters (for the standing position). The targets for the prone position will be circled with a black edge 8.75 centimeters in width (total diameter 30 centimeters).

50. Balloons used as targets shall be placed in a round cardboard sleeve 10 centimeters in length with an inside diameter of 12.5 and 30 centimeters respectively.

51. Five targets will be placed on a board as follows: two

above and two below, placed horizontally next to each other and one in the center. The distance between the five targets must be 25 centimeters minimum.

52. The distance between the boards with the targets may be 2 meters but not less than 1.5 meters.

53. Each firing lane from the firing point to the target will be marked by an adequate number of small flags or pegs.

54. A special place shall be arranged at the firing point for the sixth to eighth cartridge.

55. Replacement targets may be available in the butts, which can be raised immediately, or replacement targets marked with an *R* erected to the left and right of the roll of targets destined for competition. These boards will have four targets, two above for firing from the standing and two below for firing from the prone position.

EQUIPMENT

56. All members of the team are to dress alike and wear identical numbers.

57. At least sixteen rounds of ammunition will be carried; reserve ammunition may be carried. Lead bullets are not to be used.

58. Rules 9, 10, 11, 13, and 14 also apply to the Biathlon relay race.

SHOOTING POSITIONS

59. Rules 15 and 16 also apply to the Biathlon relay race.

COURSE PROCEDURES

60. Teams are to consist of four members. If a member of a team is unable to start, a substitute may run in his place, provided that the substitution is notified to the race committee at least half an hour before the start.

61. Team captains may decide the order of running within their teams. If they wish to, they may change this order during

the race, but no member of a team may start more than once.

62. The start is to be simultaneous for all teams and is to be made by flag or shot. If the starter rules that a false start has taken place, there is to be a fresh start.

63. Rules 17, 19, 23, 24, 25, 26, 27, and 28 also apply to the Biathlon relay race.

64. The hand over is to take place inside the relay zone, which is to be a rectangle 30 meters long and about 5 meters wide. To effect the hand over, the arriving skier must touch the starting skier on the shoulder with his hand.

65. In the case of a false hand over, the two competitors in question are to be recalled into the relay zone by the hand-over judge in order to effect a correct hand over.

66. Those who omit running the penalty rounds after firing from the prone position may run them immediately after firing the standing position and, in any case, prior to the changeover or before crossing the finishing line.

67. Competitors are responsible for running the correct number of penalty rounds.

68. A team may be disqualified if any member commits an infraction of the rules.

RANGE PROCEDURES

69. Rules 32 and 34 also apply to the Biathlon relay race.

70. On arrival at the firing point, the competitor will go to the position indicated by the firing point officer.

71. The first five cartridges may be loaded at once, the remaining three will be loaded one at a time and each one fired before the next is loaded.

72. Each competitor will fire up to eight cartridges at each stage and will continue to fire until he has fired all eight cartridges or hit all five individual targets.

73. For each individual target missed by the competitor, he will run one round of the penalty loop.

74. Competitors who have not hit all five targets and have run on without having fired all eight cartridges shall be penal-

ized to run two rounds of the penalty loop for each cartridge not fired.

75. Competitors firing more than eight rounds from one position will be disqualified.

76. For hits on targets other than their own, the competitor will, for each such hit, be penalized to run one round of the penalty loop.

77. If the competitor has to fire at the replacement target, the firing point officer will indicate with his arm whether he wants him to fire at the left or right targets and whether he has to fire at the upper or lower targets. This is indicated by a board with an *R* and an arrow pointing upward or downward.

78. The replacement targets will be the last fired on by the competitor.

Scoring

79. Total elapsed time from start of the first team member to the finish of the last team member (to include range and penalty loop time) will be the total team time.

III. Protests

80. Protests must be made in writing to the race office within two hours after the posting of the disqualifications.

81. Any protests concerning the published results of the race must be made in writing to the race office by midday on the day after the results are made public.

82. The race jury will review any protests as soon as possible after they are received. Its judgment is final.

SKIERS IN UNIFORM

Not all men in the infantry march along in boots. The U.S. Army maintains ski units in the northern reaches of the country and in Alaska.

Some members of the ski units are Eskimos, others volunteers from all parts of the United States. Information about the

Skiers in uniform: *Above*, members of the "Ski-Fire Team" from Fort Wainright, Alaska, move out over a snow-covered field. *Below*, a ski patrol from Fort Lewis, Washington prepares to move across Alaska's Lake George during "Exercise Timber Line."

U.S. Army Photos

ski troops may be obtained by writing to the Yukon Command, Fort Wainwright, Alaska.

THE 1972 OLYMPIC REPORT

The United States entered the women's Nordic cross-country skiing races for the first time at Sapporo, Japan, in the 1972 Olympics.

The following summary of the results of the cross-country competition in the 1972 Olympics is reprinted by permission of the U.S. Olympic Committee:

Norway and Sweden dominated the Nordic events four years ago in Grenoble. There was no mistake about the role of the Soviet Union at Sapporo: a clean sweep of the women's cross-country events plus victories in the men's 30 kilometers and the men's relay.

Galina Koulacova, a 29-year-old Soviet schoolteacher who lives more than 600 miles from Moscow, is a dedicated and an accomplished "runner." She captured both individual women's events and handled the anchor leg on the winning 3 × 5 kilometers relay team.

Never to be forgotten was the performance of the Japanese jumpers off the 70 meters hill. Seldom has a single nation dominated the field—the host country placed men in the top three positions and thrust Yukio Kasaya into the limelight as Japan's first (and only) gold medalist in the history of the Olympic Winter Games. More than 25,000 spectators thrilled to his performance on a cold, bright Sunday afternoon high atop Mt. Teine.

In the spectacular jumping off the 90 meters hill, a young Polish daredevil, Wojciech Fortuna, 19, a 5-foot-5-inch electrician, won the first gold medal ever gained by his country in the special jumping competition. A huge crowd of about 40,000, including Crown Prince Akihito watched the jumpers during the National Foundation Day holiday.

A native of Zakopane, where there are three hills—50 meters, 70 meters, and 90 meters—on which to practice, Fortuna decried the lack of snow at home before the Olympic Games—saying that he had had fewer than 90 jumps before coming to Sapporo. On his first official jump he registered a tremendous 111 meters and hung on to first place with a 87.5 meters performance on his second jump.

Vyacheslav Vedenin, Soviet Union, grabbed off the gold medal in the 30 kilometers race and finished third in the grueling 50 kilometers and proved tougher for the journalists than for his opposing runners. The Soviet army lieutenant refused to be interviewed after both races.

For the first time the U.S.A. entered the women's Nordic events and came up with Martha Rockwell, 27, Putney, Vt., as a world class runner. Miss Rockwell placed in the top 20 in both the 5 and 10-kilometer races. In the relay race, she made up more than one minute on her Canadian adversary but could not pull the U.S.A. trio out of last place.

After an expanded development program conducted by the U.S. Ski Association, there were hopes the Nordic events competitors would improve at Sapporo. A comparison of finish places as well as the time difference or point difference between the medal winners and the U.S.A. athletes indicates a minimum of improvement, hardly discernible to the naked eye.

Women's 5 Kilometers Cross-Country

1. Galina Koulacova, USSR 17:00.50; 2. Marjatta Kajosmaa, Finland 17:05.50; 3. Helena Sikolova, Czechoslovakia 17:07.32; 4. Alevtina Olunina, USSR 17:07.40; 5. Hilkka Kuntola, Finland 17:11.67; 6. Lubov Moukhatcheva, USSR 17:12.08.

18. Martha Rockwell, USA 17:50.34; 31. Barbara Britch, USA 18:18.37; 36. Alison Owen, USA 18:54.76; 39. Margie Mahoney, USA 19:15.13. There were 44 entries, one did not start and 43 finished.

Women's 10 Kilometers Cross-Country

1. Galina Koulacova, USSR 34:17.82; 2. Alevtina Olunina, USSR 34:54.11; 3. Marjatta Kajosmaa, Finland 34:56.45; 4. Lubov Moukhatcheva, USSR 34:58.56; 5.

Helena Takalo, Finland 35:06.34; Aslaug Dahl, Norway 35:8.84.

16. Martha Rockwell, USA 36:34.22; 35. Alison Owen, USA 38:50.05; 36. Margie Mahoney, USA 39:27.95; 41. Trina Hosmer, USA 40:40.56. There were 42 entries, 41 finished the race.

Women's 3 × 5KM Relay

1. U.S.S.R. (Lubov Moukhatcheva, Alvetina Olunina, Galina Koulacova) 48:46.15; 2. Finland (Helena Takalo, Hilkka Kuntola, Marjatta Kajosmaa) 49:19.37; 3. Norway (Inger Aufles, Aslaug Dahl, Berit Moerdre Lammedal) 49:51.49; 4. German Fed. Rep. (Monika Mirklas, Ingrid Rothfuss, Michaela Endler) 50:25.61; 5. German Dem. Rep. (Gabriele Haupt, Renate Fischer, Anna Unger) 50:-28.45; 6. Czechoslovakia (Alena Bartosova, Helena Sikolova, Milena Cillerova) 51:16.16.

11. U.S.A. (Barbara Britch, Alison Owen, Martha Rockwell) 53:38.60.

There were 11 entries, all finished.

Men's 15 Kilometers Cross-Country

1. Sven-Ake Lundback, Sweden 45:28.24; 2. Fedor Simaschov, USSR 46:00.84; 3. Ivar Formo, Norway 46:-02.68; 4. Juha Mieto, Finland 46:02.74; 5. Yuri Skobov, USSR 46:04.59; 6. Axel Lesser, German Dem. Rep. 46:17.0

44. Everett Dunklee, USA 49:52.20; 54. Timothy Caldwell, USA 51:17.92; 55. Ronny Yeager, USA 51:36.54; 58. Larry Martin, USA 53:13.91. There were 64 entries, 62 started and all finished.

Men's 30 Kilometers Cross-Country

1. Vyacheslav Vedenin, USSR 1:36:31.15; 2. Paal Tydlum, Norway 1:37:25.30; 3. Johs Harviken, Norway 1:-37:32.44; 4. Gunnar Larsson, Sweden 1:37:33.72; 5. Walter Demel, German Federal Republic 1:37:45.53; 6. Fedor Simachev, USSR 1:38:22.50.

26. Michael Elliott, USA 1:43:15.03; 30. Michael Gallagher, USA 1:43:39.41; 42. Robert Gray 1:46:38.31; 53. Clark Matis, USA 1:52:18.52.
Note: 59 entries, 55 finished.

Men's 50 Kilometers Cross-Country

1. Paal Tydlum, Norway 2 hr. 43 min. 14.75 sec.; 2. Magne Myrmo, Norway 2:43:29.45; 3. V. Vedenin, USSR 2:44:0019; 4. Reidar Hjerm, Hjermstad, Norway 2:-44.14.51; 5. Walter Demel, German Fed. Rep. 2:44:-32.67; 6 Werner Geeser, Switzerland 2:44:34.13.

24. Gene Morgan, USA 2:54:01.52; 27. Everett Dunklee, USA 2:56:42.49; 33. Robert Gray, USA 3:01:15.37. Joseph McNulty, USA, did not finish.

There were 41 entries, one did not start and seven did not finish.

Men's 4 × 10KM Relay

1. U.S.S.R. (Vladimir Voronkov, Yuri Skobov, Fedor Simaschov, V. Vedenin) 2 hr. 4 min. 47.94 sec.; 2. Norway (Oddvar Braa, Paal Tydlum, Ivar Formo, Johs Harviken) 2:04:57.06; 3. Switzerland (Alfred Kalin, Albert Giger, Alois Kalin, Eduard Hauser) 2:07:00.06; 4. Sweden (Thomas Magnusson, Lars-G. Aslund, Gunnar Larsson, Sven-Ake Lundback) 2:07:03.60; 5. Finland (Hannu Taipale, Juha Mieto, Juhani Repo, Osmo Karjalainen) 2:07:50.19; 6. German Dem. Rep. (Gerd Hessler, Axel Lesser, Gerhard Grimmer, Gert-D. Klause) 2:10:-03.73.

12. U.S.A. (Timothy Caldwell, Michael Gallagher, Larry Martin, Michael Elliott) 2:14:37.28.
There were 13 entries, all finished.

Nordic Combined Event

1. Ulrich Wehling, Ger. Dem. Rep. 413.340; 2. Rauno Miettinen, Finland 405.404; 3. Karl Luck, Ger. Dem. Rep. 398.800; 4. Erkki Kilpinen, Finland 391.845; 5. Yuji Katsuro, Japan 390.200; 6. Tomas Kucera, Czechoslovakia 387.935.

21. Michael Devecka, USA 362.835; 34. James Miller, USA 334.950; 38. Teyck Weed, USA 313.605; 39. Robert Kendall, USA 303.635. There were 39 entries, all finished.

Special Jumping, 70 Meters Hill

1. Yukio Kasaya, Japan 244.2 points (jumps: 84.0m, 79.0m); 2. Akitsugu Konno, Japan 234.8 (82.5m, 79.0); 3. Siji Aochi, Japan 229.5 (83.5m, 77.5m); 4. Ingolf Mork, Norway 225.5 (78.0m, 78.0m); 5. Jiri Raska, Czechoslovakia 224.8 (78.5m, 78.0m); 6. Wojciech Fortuna, Poland 222.0 (82.0m, 76.5m).
34. Jerry Martin, USA 197.2 (76.0m, 69.5m jumps); 41. Ron Steele, USA 192.3 (75.0m, 71.5m); 50. Gregory Swor, USA 179.4 (70.5m, 67.0m); 52. Scott Berry, USA 172.0 (67.5m, 66.0m). There were 56 entries, all completed both jumps.

Special Jumping, 90 Meters Hill

1. Wojciech Fortuna, Poland 219.9 points (111.0 and 87.5 meters jump); 2. Walter Steiner, Switzerland 219.8 (103.0 and 94.0); 3. Rainer Schmidt, German Dem. Rep. 219.3 (98.5 and 101.0); 4. Tauno Kaeyhkoe, Finland 219.2 (95.0 and 100.5); 5. Manfred Wolf, German Dem. Rep. 215.1 (107.0, 89.5); 6. Garii Napalkov, USSR 210.1 (99.5, 92.0).
25. Ron Steele, USA 177.7 (86.5, 89.0); 36. Jerry Martin, USA 163.1 (89.0, 77.5); 30. Gregory Swor, USA 172.8 (80.5, 91.5); 47. Scott Berry, USA 151.7 (79.0, 81.5).

There were 55 entries, two did not finish, one did not start.

PART V

A Guide to
Ski-Touring Areas
in the United States
and Canada

A friendly dog leads these skiers along the trails at Killington, Vermont.
Killington, Vermont Photo

8

THE EASTERN STATES

SKI TRAIL INFORMATION

Listing of Touring Trails with Details of Location, Length, and Type of Terrain

Explanation of Terms Used for Ski-Touring Trails

In order to facilitate the planning of ski tours, the trails are listed according to their location and to which type of skier they are most suitable for.

Distances are shown in miles, but it must be considered that a trail requiring a great deal of climbing will require more time than a trip of equal length over gently rolling country.

Skiers are classified as follows:

Novice—a skier who can ski under good control with a good snowplow turn and can safely descend a trail of up to 10 percent gradient.

Intermediate—an experienced skier who can negotiate almost all trails and has good control on descents up to 20 percent gradient.

Expert—the very hardy type who can take any trail at reasonable speed and bushwhack through rough country.

Beginners—should only be taken on gentle fields or meadows over short distances.

CONNECTICUT

The following Connecticut areas offer pleasant ski touring over woods roads and trails in moderately hilly country with

157

some good downhill runs for the adventurous. Short or all-day trips for good novices or intermediates should be planned with the aid of the United States Geological Survey maps, for few trails or roads are marked.

COPPER HILL

Located in the Connecticut Hills outside Hartford, this ski-touring center has the acreage of the Copper Hill Country Club and surrounding lands, for unending trails. The center serves light lunches and skiers have access to the lounge. Copper Hill is well situated for those whose time is limited and the family that cannot get away every weekend to more remote mountains. For information, contact Ken Lamarre, Manager, Copper Hill Ski Touring Center, Copper Hill Country Club, Granby, Conn. 06035. Tel. 203-653-2665.

BLACKBERRY RIVER INN SKI-TOURING CENTER– ROUTE 44, NORFOLK 06058

Seven miles of well-marked beginner and intermediate trails wind through the meadows and woodlands of the Litchfield Hills, foothills of the Berkshires. For the day skier, facilities include a new, comfortable base lodge converted from an old icehouse, food, drink, and warm atmosphere. Rental and sales shop in lodge, instruction and guide service available daily. For the overnighter, ice skating, tobogganing, plus all the facilities of a New England inn. For brochure or information write, or tel. 203-542-5100.

LITCHFIELD

Suggestions for Cross-Country Skiers Using White's Woods

Although the guide map available from White Memorial Foundation (office located off Route 25 between Bantam and

158

Litchfield) shows numerous choices, the problem of wintertime parking makes some of the entry points impractical. Also, the skiing is often more pleasant if someone else has broken the trail!

The whole area is laced with well-cleared woods roads and is relatively level as a Nordic area should be. The following tours are suggested:

(a.) Enter at bottom of Gallows Lane and ski south to golf course, over the Bantam River, then into the woods where the small shelter for golfers stands.

(b.) Enter any one of three roads leading into Catlin Woods from Webster Road (dirt) and ski north and east into the golf-course area and back.

(c.) At the same point off Webster Road, enter Cranberry Woods road and ski south about .75 mile to the numerous trails which circulate through this undulating, wooded area.

(d.) Ski into this same area (c) from Big Cathedral Road, off Route 61.

(e.) If plowing permits, park near Heron Pond or Middle Woods roads. Ski east from Route 63 (junction of Route 61), where many circular routes are available.

Information: J. C. Hart, South Street, Litchfield. Tel. 203-567-9163. For waxes and equipment: Litchfield Hills Ski Shop, near corner of South Lake Street and Route 25.

PEOPLES STATE FOREST

Located in the town of Barkhamsted, east of the West Branch of the Farmington River. Access is from Connecticut Route 181, most conveniently from the East River Road running north from Pleasant Valley. An excellent map is available in the *Connecticut Walk Book*, 1972 edition, obtainable from the Connecticut Forest and Park Association, Inc., PO Box 389, East Hartford, Conn. 06108.

MIDDLEFIELD

Powder Ridge Ski Area, Off Route 66, Between Middletown and Meriden

Powder Ridge has the Mattabassett Trail, a portion of the Blue Trail system, running in a north-south direction from the top of the mountain. Novice, intermediate, and expert trails to 15 miles through the Connecticut countryside. Ski equipment, rentals, and lessons are available at the area, as well as chair lifts for those not desiring a 2,600-foot climb to the trail system. Short trips and all-day tours are featured throughout the season. Call Al Benton at 203-349-3454, for information about ski touring.

SALISBURY

This is an intermediate trail with a great variety of terrain and views. It starts a few miles from the center of town, gently climbs for a few miles, then after passing the Revolutionary War ironworks and a lakeshore, the trail enters several miles of upland woods crossing into Egremont, Massachusetts. The entire trail is 8 miles, more or less, but you can turn back sooner and finish with a gentle and wide downhill run.

At Route 44 in Salisbury, turn north at the Town Hall and follow the road toward Mounts Riga and Washington. Park at the end of the plowed road. Snow lasts here until very late spring. Salisbury is a well-known Nordic skiing area, and most of the snowmobilers are courteous; but nonetheless keep an ear open for them. Details from PO Box 103, Concord, Mass. 01742.

SHARON

Sharon Audubon Center, Sharon, Connecticut, 11066

A 526-acre wildlife sanctuary. Open Tuesday–Saturday, 9 to 5; Sunday, 1 to 5. Closed Mondays and holidays or holiday

160

weekends. Several short trails (longest approximately 2 miles) through deciduous-coniferous forest and upland meadows. Suitable for beginners and up. Excellent views. All visitors are requested to check in at the center for map and trail information. Request brochure describing the center. Also, ski-touring trips for those interested in learning more about forest and fields in winter.

TUNXIS STATE FOREST AND ADJOINING GRANVILLE STATE FOREST

Located in the town of Hartlands, east of the Barkhamsted Reservoir. Access from Connecticut Routes 179 and 20. Granville State Forest is located in Granville and Tolland, Mass., and adjoins the Tunxis Forest on the north.

THE MOUNT RIGA PLATEAU

A relatively inaccessible area located in the towns of Salisbury, Conn., and Mount Washington, Mass. In winter the only access is by the Mount Washington Road, starting south from Egremont, Mass., or by Route 344 from Copake, N.Y. The drive should not be attempted by those unfamiliar with mountain roads in winter. Cars may be left at Whitbeck's Farm at the end of plowed road. Map of Connecticut portion obtainable from Norman D. Sills, Salisbury, Conn.

The Connecticut Forest and Park Association has available a booklet, *The Connecticut Walk Book*, which includes description of the 500 miles of blue-blazed hiking trails in Connecticut, most of which are suitable for cross-country ski touring. There are some areas that are too steep, but if topographic maps are used in conjunction with the walk book, these problem areas can easily be avoided. For a copy of the book write John E. Hibbard, Secretary, Forester, Connecticut Forest and Park Association, Inc., 1010 Main Street, PO Box 389, East Hartford, Conn. 06108.

MAINE

Acadia National Park, Mount Desert Island

Park open all year. Lodging and meals in the town of Bar Harbor. Blackwoods Campground open, no running water November to April. Excellent ski touring and snowshoeing on the 40-mile carriage-path system. Best season, January to March. For information call 207-288-3338, or write Superintendent, Acadia National Park, Route 1, Box 1, Bar Harbor, Maine 04609.

Andover, Farrington Hill Trails

Start 200 yards up Church Street from Route 5, 100 yards south of the grammar school, or at Akers Ski. Trail runs through soft woods over rolling terrain in a westerly direction for .8 miles; at this point a right turn takes you downhill and back to the point of beginning, not crossing any highways, .6 mile. A left turn takes you uphill to a small clearing, where another left turn takes you on the marked trail, about 1.8 miles through timbered forest, except for the last .4 mile, which is open, owing to being recently cut over, back to start.

Trails are well marked and have been used for racing for many years. Intermediate to expert. Beginners should follow trail backward for 1 mile and return.

Booby Town Road

Start 1 mile south of Andover Village, across from the cemetery. This old logging road is nearly flat for the first mile, where it connects briefly with the Farrington Hill Trail. Continuing westward another .5 mile, the road starts up Long Mountain, where it winds upward for about another mile, providing a view of the valley and Telstar tracking station.

Andover-Crocker Bridge. Approximately 3 miles.
Intermediate to Expert

Start the same as Farrington Hill Trails. Upon reaching the opening at the top of Farrington Hill, continue straight and bear a bit right. The next .5 mile is mostly easy downhill. When you reach level ground, you follow an old logging road over rolling terrain bearing right (about 1.5 miles), emerging on the Upton Road near Crocker Bridge. A sharp left, .25 mile before reaching the road will take you to the Stony Brook Trail (approximately .5 mile).

Stony Brook–Grafton Notch

A continuous trip can be made from Andover to Stony Brook to Grafton Notch to Chase Hill Pastures to Gardiner Brook and back to Andover, which amounts to 25 to 30 miles, and all but the last 3 miles along Route 5 are in woods.

To shorten the trip, start at Stony Brook, 2.5 miles west of Andover, on the Upton Road. The start is approximately at the 800-foot level and climbs about 800 feet in the first 1.5 miles along an old logging road. It then levels into a very gentle upgrade as you move up the valley, finally pitching over the Grafton Notch side after approximately 4 miles and an elevation of about 2,200 feet. At this point only experts should continue on, as the terrain is rough and in places the only trail has been made by snowmobiles. The trail drops several hundred feet before climbing back to about the same elevation and pitching back to the Andover side in Gardiner Valley, then following an old logging road out to intersection Route 5, 3 miles south of Andover.

East B Hill Road

This road usually is not plowed through to Upton in the winter. There could be 6 to 10 miles unplowed road through the wilderness. The first 3 miles, above the Appalachian Trail, is only slightly upgrade. The next 3 miles climb about 800 feet.

This is a paved road except for a section at the very top, thus providing a wide trail with gentle turns.

Surplus Pond

Follow the Appalachian Trail north from Upton Road, on an old logging road. The first .5 mile or so is flat and a little rolling. The next 3 miles climb about 1,000 feet to the small pond (approximately .25 mile across). OK for intermediates.

Surplus Pond–C Pond–Andover

Continue on the Appalachian Trail from Surplus Pond 3–4 miles downgrade about 700 feet to C Pond (1.5 miles long), and then about 2.5 miles east to the shelter. There are a couple of short, steep pitches in this section. Near the trail shelter leave the Appalachian Trail, and continue southeast 5 miles of rolling terrain along an old logging road through Sawyer Notch (cliffs rise about 1,200 feet above you here). Then, on down Sawyer Brook to meet the town road about 3 miles north of town.

Sawyer Notch

Follow the above trail backward as far as you care to go toward C Pond (approximately 8 miles). This makes an excellent trail for the family.

Merrill Bridge–Sawyer Brook

Start at the end of the road which goes upriver .25 mile on the east side of the river at Merrill Bridge (.25 mile east of Andover on Route 5). After a short stretch of woods go downhill into a field and more northerly .5 to .75 miles past farm buildings and more field, then into gently rolling terrain in the woods until you reach the town road near Sawyer Brook, 2 to 3 miles (you can continue from here toward Sawyer Notch).

Baldpate Valley-Mountain

Start south on the Appalachian Trail where it crosses the Upton Road. The first 2 miles consist of easy climbs and flats or slight grades and rise about 1,000 feet along a logging road. Then, as the trail becomes steep, only experts should continue. If your intentions are to reach the peak of Baldpate (just under 4,000 feet), you should go well prepared, as you may find several conditions ranging from ice to powder. You will not be able to do much actual skiing, as you will find the terrain steep until you near the top, but rather, you will walk on your skis. However, if conditions permit klister (as in the spring) you may find this is the easiest way to proceed, even if you do not need the skis for support. (Take your ski poles regardless.) The top of this mountain is clear of trees and provides one of the best views of any mountain in the East, stretching from the Atlantic Ocean to mountains more distant than Mount Washington.

Wyman Mountain-Surplus Pond-Upton Road.
Expect, 6 to 7 Miles

Start 3 miles north of Andover at the base of Wyman Hill, follow an old logging road uphill through the field continuing into the woods and upward for approximately 1.5 miles. At this point the trunk road ends, and you take the left skidder road, climbing steeply for another mile. After climbing about 1,500 feet (total), you are nearing the crest (not the top of the mountain) of the climb and a section with little trail for perhaps .5 mile. Then you pitch over toward Surplus Pond in a northwesterly direction and drop 300 to 400 feet in a little over a mile to the pond, then continue downhill along the Appalachian Trail south to the Upton Road.

Ellis River, West Branch

Start at east side of river at Crocker Bridge, 2 miles west of Andover on the Upton Road, following the trail up along the river over rolling terrain about 2 miles. All woods except field at the start.

Ellis River–Abbott Brook

Start at the same place as above. Go in northerly direction; slight upgrade for about 1.5 miles through woods.

Notes on Andover Trails

A very few of the trails described may have logging operations on sections of the trail. In good weather you get a fine view from many points on most trails. Andover is situated in a valley completely surrounded by mountains averaging about 2,800 feet above sea level. This helps in keeping your bearings. There are many other trails. Among these are Black Mountain Road to Relay Station, Whitecap Mountain (free of trees, also looks onto Rumford), and South Arm Road to Garland Pond (not plowed in winter).

CORNVILLE

Hilton Hill is planning ski-touring trails on its 250-acre property. For information, contact Barbara Harthorn, Hilton Hill, Skowhegan, Maine 04976.

FRYEBURG

Fryeburg has an excellent 8-mile racing trail as well as a downhill slope and a jump (snowmobiles are kept to a special trail).

KINGFIELD–SUGARLOAF MOUNTAIN CORPORATION

Sugarloaf Mountain ski areas offer four trails covering more than 20 miles and three additional trails covering 9 miles which were used for the NCAA Championships in 1968. Additional trails are being planned for future seasons. Instructions, rentals, and sales of equipment available. Area organizes lunch tours. For information: Sugarloaf Mountain Corporation, Kingfield, Maine 04947. Tel. 207-237-2601.

Located 6 miles north of Bridgton, Maine, at the junction of state roads 35 and 37. A year-round facility with several winterized, heated cottages for winter occupancy. Heavily wooded, hilly, and mountainous terrain and rurally located. Back road and old logging trails adjoining the property afford scenic and interesting short cross-country skiing trips. Use of cottages and main lodge as a base accommodation for a week or by the weekend. Large or small day groups are welcome. Reservations a MUST. Equipment is available at nearby ski area in Bridgton. Most unusual attraction to ski touring is old logging road to the top of Hawk Mountain—2 miles each way—approximately one-half day's ski touring. Owned and operated by Dave and Teddy Erickson, Star Route, Harrison, Maine 04040. Tel. 207-583-2541.

MARYLAND

Ski-tour conditions occur in Garrett County, where unplowed forest roads, logging roads, and firebreaks afford best ski opportunities in Savage River State Forest and adjacent New Germany State Park. Trails and breaks may also be used at Swallow Falls and Herrington Manor state parks and Potomac State Forest in Allegany County. Current information available from state park superintendents and district foresters.

Although the snow conditions are not consistently good and trails are not wide, the Catoctin Mountain National Park (which surrounds the President's Camp David) offers good ski touring. Catoctin and Cunningham Falls are within Sunday afternoon round-trip range from both Baltimore and Washington and, for the more ambitious, from Philadelphia.

MASSACHUSETTS

HOLYOKE

This ski-touring center is located in the Connecticut River

Valley, on the grounds of the Wycoff Park Country Club. This land, plus surrounding areas, leads to an unlimited trail system. The Nordic specialty shop located in the clubhouse offers cross-country equipment and accessories, a complete line of rental gear, ski instruction, and guided tours. This center will also serve light lunches and skiers have access to the lounge. Contact John Tidd, Manager, Holyoke Ski Touring Center, Holyoke, Mass. 01040, Wycoff Park Country Club. Tel. 413-532-7805.

TACONIC RANGE

Suitable for good novices and intermediate skiers.

Petersburg Pass–Berlin Mountains–Berlin

Start from Petersburg Pass (2,090 feet) on the Taconic Trail (Route 2) between Petersburg, N.Y., and Williamstown, Mass. (Petersburg Pass Ski Area). From the top of the lift go down on the south side for several hundred feet and pick up the Taconic Crest Trail (white blazes on trees). Go south along trail for 1.5 miles to open meadows at Berlin Pass. The trail enters the woods after 1.2 miles at an easy grade, reaches Berlin Mountain (2,798 feet) with magnificent views. (Good place for lunch.) Here you may run down the college ski area (about 1,100 feet, rather steep trail and slope); climb back on old Berlin Road (rises about 600 feet in 2,200 feet) to Berlin Pass; or, you may take the trail back via Berlin Pass to Petersburg Pass (distance 2.7 miles).

Or, if you have left your car in Berlin, you can go west on Berlin Pass (old Boston–Albany Post Road) down Greene Hollow for a pleasant run of about 2 miles. Purchase:

> *Williams Outing Club Guide*
> PO Box 627, Williamstown, Mass.
> Price 75 cents.

HANCOCK

Tower Mountain Lodge, near Stephenstown, N.Y., off Route

22. For information: Art Jensen, Tower Mountain Lodge, Hancock, Mass. 01237.

Hoosac Range Circuit

On the high plateau of Hoosac Mountain, southeast of North Adams, there is excellent high-level cross-country terrain and circuits used by the Williams College cross-country team. Take the Mohawk Trail east out of North Adams to the fork, about .3 mile beyond the West Summit where Strykers Road branches off to the right. Continue on this about 2.5 miles to Shaft Road, and right on it about 1 mile to North Pond.

Pittsfield State Forest

This extensive tract in the towns of Pittsfield, Hancock, and Lanesboro is laid out with skiers (downhill and cross-country and jumpers) specifically in mind, and all facilities are maintained in excellent condition. Access is from West Street, Pittsfield, Mass. The Taconic Skyline Trail, much of which is skiable, crosses the forest, circuits up to 10 miles in length and of varying difficulty may be laid out. A forest map is obtainable from the Commonwealth of Massachusetts Department of Conservation.

South Egremont–Jug End Resort

Two miles southwest of the intersection of Routes 23 and 41, in the southern end of the Berkshire Hills of western Massachusetts. Network of horse trails through scenic Guilder Hollow, located on the resort's grounds, varying from 2 to 8 miles in length. Interesting for the good skier and challenging for the novices. The golf course is used for instruction. The resort has a snack bar, and box lunches are available. Leader: Ralph Beers. Tel. 413-528-0434.

NEW HAMPSHIRE

ACWORTH

Acworth Town contains more than 25 miles of old abandoned roads, jeep roads, suitable for all levels of ski-touring ability, through woods, open fields, steep hills, rolling hills, level areas, etc. Accommodations and meals available at the Acworth Cross Country Inn, equipment for rent and sale. For information write or call John or Mary Clarke, Box 85, Acworth, N.H. 03601. Tel. 603-835-6869.

BREEZY POINT

The Carriage Road begins at Breezy Point, the location of the Moosilauke Inn. It is 5.1 miles to the summit. At no time is it too steep for properly waxed skis to ascend or for an intermediate ski tourer to descend without undue terror. It is wider than most hiking trails. Excellent views.

The full trip should not be attempted in midwinter as winds on the ridge make for severe conditions. The hut on the summit is available for temporary shelter. The average party should allow 4 hours for ascent.

The trail is well marked by orange blazes. It joins the Glencliff hiking trail at 2.8 miles, then ascends more steeply for 2,300 feet with many switchbacks, and passes the Snapper Ski Trail, leading right to the Dartmouth Ravine Lodge.

This is bordering on ski mountaineering in the sense that it would appeal to those who like to get out of the valleys and gain altitude when the weather gets better.

FRANCONIA

Franconia is an active ski center and additional facilities are planned for ski tourers. The touring center is located at the Franconia Inn. Contact Audre Dunklee, Manager, Franconia Ski Touring Center, Franconia Inn, Franconia, N.H. 03580. Tel. 603-823-8877.

GRANTHAM

Grey Ledges

For information call Mrs. Carol A. Sturgis, 603-863-9880.
Suitable for novices and intermediates. Approximately 10
miles of trails over rolling, somewhat hilly countryside. The
trails begin at Grey Ledges Lodge, high on a mountain at
Grantham. The trails are well marked and follow tote roads and
pathways throughout 1,000 acres of land. Snowmobiles not
permitted on touring trails.

GREELEY POND TRAIL

Kancamagus Highway to Waterville Valley, 6 miles. Intermediate. Trail goes up to Greeley Ponds and then down to
Waterville Valley. Offers many miles of excellent ski touring,
good grades, and fine views. The trail starts on the Kancamagus
Highway, about 5 miles east of Loon Mountain. Not used by
snowmobiles.

CARRIGAN NOTCH–SAWYER POND AREA

This is an extensive area of roads, logging roads, and trails
which start at the Sawyer River Road, Hart's Location at the
southern end of Crawford Notch, off Route 302. Two trips
recommended:

(1) Carrigan Notch. Six miles, steep climb 1,600 feet. Intermediate–expert. Take the Sawyer River Road for 2 miles to
the Signal Ridge Trail. Follow the Signal Ridge Trail up through
a beautiful brook gully for about 1 mile to the intersection of the
main logging road crossing the trail. Follow the logging road
north up through the Carrigan Brook Valley. Ar the end of
logging road bear left, cross brook and pick up Carrigan Notch
Trail just across brook. Easy grades except for the last mile up to
the Notch. Return via logging road or via Carrigan Notch Trail.
Not extensively used by snowmobiles. Because of old logging

operations in the area, there are unobstructed views of the steep Carrigan Notch and Mount Lowell from the logging road.

(2) Sawyer Pond. Five miles. Intermediate. 1,200-foot vertical climb. This trip starts at the Sawyer River Road and terminates at Sawyer Pond. Follow this road for 4 miles to the Sawyer Pond Trail. Follow the Sawyer Pond Trail 1 mile to Sawyer Pond. Excellent grades for ski touring. Area is used by snowmobiles. From Sawyer Pond you may return to start or continue on to Kancamagus Highway.

HENNIKER–POLE AND PEDAL SHOP

Miles of maintained trails directly from shop in center of town, equipment rentals, sales, and instruction. Specializing in touring and 10-speed bicycles. Co-owner Peter Davis is member of past and present U.S. Nordic teams. Contact Pole and Pedal Shop, Box 327, Henniker, N.H. 03242.

JACKSON–JACKSON SKI-TOURING FOUNDATION

A unique program combining the joint efforts of Jackson Valley region residents, ski areas, inns, and ski shops coordinated through the touring center in the village. Seventy-five miles of prepared touring trails interconnecting all the inns and ski areas includes a 10-mile run from the summit of Wildcat to Jackson Village. Daily classes at 10 A.M. and 1:30 P.M. Two or more guided tours per week, several clinics. Shuttle bus between North Conway, Jackson area, and Wildcat Mountain. Map available. Complete rentals, sales, and instruction available, plus accommodations, information, and reservations. Included below are directions for skiing seven of the more popular trails. Those desiring further information, contact Jackson Ski Touring Foundation, Jackson, N.H. Tel. 603-383-9355.

1. Mirror Lake Trail: Novice, .75 Mile

The trail starts at the rear of the ski-touring center and crosses the Wildcat River; turns left and follows the golf-course perimeter clockwise to the Wildcat Valley Country Store; crosses the road and follows the golf course to its northwest corner where it enters the woods on the right; then climbs gradually for .2 mile to the lake.

2. Dana Place Trail: Novice, 1.5 Miles

Four miles north of the village of Jackson at Dana Place the trail starts at the front door; passing through the orchard to the south of the inn, the trail enters the woods, crosses the Ellis River on a cable suspension bridge into a series of open pastures, then through thick spruce along the riverside to an old farmsite where there is a cabin with fireplace for shelter. Return to Dana Place is via the same route.

3. Black Mountain Valley Trails: Novice–Intermediate, 2 Miles

These trails provide some great panoramic views of the White Mountains and Mount Washington through a series of meandering interconnected pastures. The trails start at Whitney's Inn, 1 mile above Jackson Village on the Black Mountain Road. Beginner's Loop, 1 mile; Davis Loop, 1 mile.

4. Great Brook Trail: Novice–Intermediate, 2 Miles

The trail starts near the beginning of Dundee Road by Black Mountain Tramways, entering a field on the left; climbs to the top of the field and enters the treeline on the left; In .25 mile it intersects an old logging road, turns left, which it follows to a field. From the highest point in the field it enters the woods, in about .1 mile intersects the East Pasture Trail, continues to climb gradually, then descends to the Sugar Bush Trail on Black Mountain, and on to the base of Black Mountain Tramways, completing a loop to the starting point.

5. Jackson Village Trail: Intermediate, 1.25 Miles

From the rear of the Wildcat Tavern in Jackson Village, the

trails enters the woods on the right, climbs to a small field, bears right at the other end of the field, and enters the woods again. The trail then loops counterclockwise to the foot of the old Thorn Mountain Ski Area along two unmaintained roads. The trip back to the village is downhill with several steep runs. Use caution.

6. *East Pasture Trail: Intermediate–Expert 2.5 Miles*

This trail departs from the end of Black Mountain Road, 1.5 miles above Jackson Village; intersects the Great Brook Trail after 300 yards; bears left at the fork with the Bald Land Trail, then climbs quite continuously along an old road through several fields to the ridgeline of Black Mountain. From here the skier may descend the west side to the Black Mountain Ski Trail and cabin or climb to the right to the old Davis Tower site.

7. *Prospect Farm Trail: All Abilities, 2 Miles*

Four miles north of Jackson Village, at the end of Carter Notch Road, the trail begins. It follows an old roadway bearing left at the intersection with the Bog Brook Trail, then up to the Prospect Farm site. From here, many old logging roads depart with magnificent views of Mount Washington and the Presidential Range.

Future plans include a trail system about 75 miles in length, completely interconnected and including nine inns and three major ski areas as well as the village. Trails will run from beginner's loops to first-class wilderness excursions into the national forest. A full-time trail maintenance crew will be employed. The trail system will also incorporate a shuttle-bus service and several overnight cabins, also a new ski-touring shop.

Loon Mountain Ski Area, Lincoln

Rentals and instruction are available at the ski area. Black Mountain Road 2 miles, beginner, starts at base lodge of ski area. For free map of touring trails inquire at ticket office. The

Black Mountain Road also connects with the Wilderness Trail, which offers many miles of ski touring following logging railroad beds in the Pemigewasset Wilderness. Used by snowmobilers.

ZEALAND NOTCH, TWIN MOUNTAIN

Beginner–expert. Eight miles from Route 302 to the Notch. One thousand-foot vertical climb. Go 3.5 miles on Forest Service road. The remainder is an attractive trail with rolling terrain and fairly level. Used by snowmobiles to the notch. The notch is impassable by snowmobiles. Beyond it there is an extensive system of hiking trails in the Pemigewasset Wilderness. The shortest route out from Zealand Notch to the south is the Ethan Pond Trail to the Willey House Station. Fairly level terrain except for the last .5 mile, which is a steep downgrade hill. Distance from Zealand Notch to the Willey House is 6 miles. This is along the Appalachian Trail. There are no snowmobiles. Longer trips out via Carrigan Notch to the Sawyer River Road or Wilderness Trail to Kancamagus Highway are suitable for a two-day trip. Purchase the Appalachian Mountain Club map, "Franconia Region," $1 from the Appalachian Mountain Club, 5 Joy Street, Boston, Massachusetts 02108 or at ski shops in the White Mountains Region.

CRAWFORD NOTCH

Beginner–Expert. Twenty-four miles of unplowed roads offer easy touring and unsurpassed views of Mount Washington. The road opposite the Crawford House gives access to Edmund's Path and to the Cog Railroad Base Station. Ski mountaineering is possible on the Cog Railroad right-of-way up to timberline. Also, the Cog Railroad Base Road starts at Bretton Woods, 6 miles to the Cog Railroad Base. In addition, there is the Jefferson Notch Road, 12 miles long, climbing up to 3,000 feet at Jefferson Notch. This area is extensively used by snowmobiles, particularly on weekends.

175

MOUNT WILLARD, CRAWFORD NOTCH

Intermediate. There are 1.4 miles of short trip with an outstanding view of Crawford Notch. The Mount Willard Trail follows the old carriage road up Mount Willard. Some steep pitches. Starts at the western end of the Crawford House on the railroad overpass at the Avalon Trail.

FRANCONIA–MITTERSILL AREA

A trail called the Old Road is about 4 miles long and is ideal for touring. Also, there is a 5-mile loop starting at Lafayette Campground which is used by cross-country racers. This is an excellent trail with many fine views of the mountains and cliffs in the area. The trail does, however, require 12 inches of snow in order to be skiable. Snowmobiles excluded. Beginner–intermediate.

Franconia Notch State Park Trail System

The system is 5.1 miles in length over state and U.S. forest land—over old U.S. Route 3 and links up woods roads from logging operations of long ago. The main parking lot is at Echo Lake, where the trail system begins. Parking is also available at the northern end of the trail system. There is no charge for use of the trails. Instructions and ski rentals are available at the Peabody Slopes Building. Trail maps available. Wear light, windproof clothing. Carry a heavier parka if you plan extended stops such as picnics.

PINKHAM NOTCH AREA

Ski-touring trails information supplied by Appalachian Mountain North Country System, Pinkham Notch Camp, Gorham, N.H. 03581. Tel. 603-466-3994.

Blanchard Loop. Approximately 1 Mile

This trail bears right from the John Sherburne Ski Trail about

100 feet from the Pinkham Notch parking lot. It continues a short distance to the site of a new staff residence house near the lodge building, then bears left along the route of an old water-pipe. It soon reaches the bank of the Cutler River, then the Tuckerman Ravine Trail, going left in conjunction with this trail for some 200 yards, then turning right on an old logging road. It descends moderately, then more gently; crosses the Old Jackson Road, then descends by gentle grades to Route 16, about 200 yards north of Pinkham Notch Camp. Circuits of various lengths may be made from this camp by turning right on the Tuckerman Ravine Trail, Old Jackson Road, and Route 16. In general, the section south of the Tuckerman Trail is more easily negotiated, although the entire length may be utilized by novices. Grade of difficulty: Novice. (Recommended for novice training and beginner practice.) Marking: Green disks.

Thompson Falls to Glenn House. Approximately 2.5 Miles

This route diverges left from the Thompson Falls Trail at a point about 200 feet below the lower falls. It descends slightly, crosses Thompson Brook, then ascends slightly to a junction with the power line serving Wildcat and Pinkham Notch Camp. It follows the power line, rising and falling somewhat with the slope, being in general downhill to the Glen House. One steep section near the north end of the route may require sidestepping for about 300 feet in each direction. The route diverges left from the power line at a marked tree and follows a recent logging road to the south end of the Glen House, clearing about 300 feet from Route 16. In returning, look for marked trees in the southeast corner of the Glen House field, turn right from the logging road into the power line, then watch for marked trees indicating the left turn for the connecting link to Thompson Falls Trail.

Grade of difficulty: Advanced beginner. Marking: Plastic tape at junctions. Note that this route allows a circuit trip using the Jackson Road, Auto Road, power line, and Thompson Falls Trail and Pinkham Notch Ski Trail.

Lost Pond Trail. *Approximately 1 Mile*

This trail leaves Route 16 at a point slightly south of the Pinkham Notch Camp. The summer trail crosses the Ellis River on a bridge, but in times of deep snow it is possible to cross the swamp directly, striking the trail on the east bank. The trail turns hard right at the east end of the bridge and follows the east bank of the river for .3 mile. (Caution: Don't ski on overhanging snow near the river.) It then ascends slightly to the north end of Lost Pond. The summer trail continues straight on the east bank of the pond, but the skiing route follows the west bank on snow-covered ice (when safe), crosses the beaver dam at the outlet, bears slightly left, and rejoins the summer trail. Almost immediately there is a steep stretch that may require sidestepping for some 75 feet. The trail soon joins the Wildcat Ridge Trail, turning right for Route 16 at Glen Ellis parking lot. Use caution in crossing the Ellis River at this point. Grade of difficulty: Beginner. Marking: Plastic tape.

Mount Washington Auto Road (8 Miles)

This road is not recommended for ski travel above treeline, as high winds, low temperatures, and ice make it extremely dangerous for any but experienced winter mountaineers. However, the lower 4 miles from treeline at the Halfway House to the base at the Glen House provide excellent skiing for advanced skiers, with only a little snow. The road is at its best just after a light snowfall which covers icy spots and ruts left by snow machines. A fine circuit trip is possible using the old Jackson Road and the Auto Road. Ascend the old Jackson Road, turn left on the Auto Road, and follow it for a short distance to where the Madison Gulf Trail leaves right. Follow this for about .25 mile to the open summit of Lowe's Bald Spot (fine views). Skis may be left for the short scramble to the top. Descend to the Glen House by the Auto Road. A link is available from the Glen House to Wildcat Ski Area, allowing a return by the Pinkham Notch Ski Trail. Grade of difficulty: Beginner. Marking: Not needed.

Pinkham Notch Ski Trail and Thompson Falls (1.3 Miles)

This trail leave Route 16 at a point slightly north of Pinkham Notch Camp, crosses a swamp and a small stream, and bears left into the woods on a prominent logging road. It ascends gently to a second stream, soon bears left near an old practice slope, continues to ascend for about .2 mile, then drops sharply to a third stream, passing the base of the old Wildcat Racing Trail and Timer's Hut. It ascends again, soon reaching the runout of the southernmost of the Wildcat ski runs. To reach Thompson Falls, descend the runout to the Main Lodge and Gondola Base Station. (Caution: Watch for fast-moving downhill skiers.) Descend slightly, and turn right into a service road near a small stream. Follow this to some maintenance buildings, passing them on the left; then follow an abandoned section of Route 16 to the south end of a concrete highway bridge. Turn right at a marked tree for the short ascent to the lower falls. An alternate route to bypass the swamp is available. It begins on the Lost Pond Trail some 200 feet from the bridge over the Ellis River at the north end of the trail. It ascends quite steeply for a few yards, then becomes level, passes to the east of Ladies' Lodge, then descends slightly to the base of an old practice slope near Square Lodge. To rejoin the Pinkham Notch Ski Trail, descend a short stretch of prominent logging road, turn right for Wildcat and Thomspon Falls. When returning, turn left at the base of a prominent clearing. Distance: Pinkham Notch Camp to Wildcat Ski Area, .6 mile; concrete bridge, 1 mile; Thompson Falls, 1.3 miles. Grade difficulty: Advanced beginner. Marking: Plastic tape at junctions. Alternate distance: .4 mile, advanced beginner. Marking: Plastic tape.

Old Jackson Road (1.64 Miles)

This trail leaves Pinkham Notch Camp some 200 feet from the lower end of the Tuckerman Ravine Trail. It winds through the woods for about .2 mile, crossing the base of the Snowcat Road and then a small stream. It then ascends somewhat steeply for about .5 mile, crossing two streams, then levels out through some attractive woods, crosses a third stream, and ascends to the Auto Road at the 2-mile point. Grade of difficulty: Beginners ascending; intermediate descending. Markings: Plastic tape at junctions.

Gulf of Slides Trail. Suitable Only for Expert Skiers

This trail is maintained by the White Mountain National Forest. A winding trail leaves Pinkham Notch Highway, No. 16, 100 yards south of Appalachian Mountain Club camp. Ascends 2,200 feet in 2.5 miles to the bowl of the Gulf of Slides. Skiable until May. The bowl is gentler and more evenly graded, suitable for intermediates, and a challenge to experts, depending on inclination and ability of the skier. Beautiful views, enough open spots to slalom and stop. Requires downhill equipment.

WILDERNESS SKI AREA, DIXVILLE NOTCH

Intermediate. From the top of the chair lift there is a jeep road going to the summit of Dixville Peak, about a 1,000-foot climb in 2 miles through large spruce, fir growth. This northern area has exceptionally heavy snow so there is a good place to find snow when other areas are bare. Used by snowmobiles.

The White Mountains Ski Touring Club, a new ski-touring club, has been organized in the White Mountains Region, open to all. The club takes trips three times a month, mostly for beginners or intermediates. The trips are planned on a monthly basis. Those interested in receiving a free monthly bulletin of trip schedules may do so by writing to the White Mountains Region Association, Lancaster, N.H. 03584. Tel. 1-603-788-2061.

Ski shops renting touring equipment:

Carroll Reed Shop, North Conway, Loon Mountain, and Franconia
Jack Frost Shop, Jackson
Appalachian Mountain Club, Pinkham Notch

MOUNT MOOSILAUKE

This area is owned by Dartmouth College. Recommended trip is the Entrance Road at Dartmouth's Ravine Lodge, 6.75 miles northeast of Warren, on Route 118, 2 miles in length. From there is a system of ski trails for all abilities. No snowmobiles. Contact Director of Ski Touring, Dartmouth Outdoor Club, Robinson Hall, Hanover, N.H. 03755, for free map. Cabins are available.

NEW IPSWICH 03071–WINDBLOWN–
1½ HOURS FROM BOSTON

Ski-touring area primarily designed to provide first-timers with experience. There are several miles of meandering trails in woodlands and a warming hut. The warming hut offers overnight lodging with sleeping bags. Wood furnished for heating fire. There are also trails for more experienced skiers. One of the trails leads to the summit with an excellent view of the Nonodnock region—for more experienced skiers. Longer tours may be arranged. Maps available. Equipment for rent and sale and instruction available. Food must be brought along. Because of limited capacity (30 to 40 people) in the hut, advance reservations must be made. Dogs and other friendly animals are welcome. For details write Al Jenks, RFD, New Ipswich, N.H. 03071.

PLYMOUTH: TENNEY MOUNTAIN CORPORATION, BOX 11

Maintains a 2.5-mile loop of ski-touring trails on the top of Tenney Mountain, which is reached by a 6,000-foot double chair. Instructions, rentals, and sales available.

TEMPLE MOUNTAIN SKI AREA, INC.
ROUTE 101, PETERBOROUGH 03458. TEL. 603-924-6949

Touring and Alpine season December 10 to April 15. Ski-area elevation 1,486 to 1,904 feet. Annual snowfall 100 to 150 inches. Touring instruction, guided tours, rentals, and sales available. Trail maps available at Temple Mountain Ski Shop.

WOLFEBORO

Miles of trails through scenic countryside. Marked trails being developed. Golf course, trails, follow along edge of woods. Novice, intermediate, and experts will find ideal areas to tour. Active local ski patrol and Nordic ski club. Motels and inns also promoting touring. Headquarters for touring information, ski rentals, sales, and instructors are at the Nordic Skier in downtown Wolfeboro.

For information write or call Cal Flagg, PO Box 297, Clow Road, Wolfeboro, N.H. 03894. Tel. 603-569-3151.

NEW JERSEY

McAFEE. GREAT GORGE SKI AREA. TEL. 201-827-9146

All touring trails start and end at the Summit Lodge, to be reached by lift. The trails are up to 10 miles in length with an expert section that is 3.1 miles long. The trails run through the Hamburg Mountain Game Preserve, and at points along the way, excellent views can be enjoyed. There is also a novice trail of 2 miles. At the summit there is a snack bar. In order to reach Summit Lodge area, charge is $6 for lift.

PALISADES PARK, NEAR NEW YORK CITY

Coming from New York, take George Washington Bridge, turn north into Palisades Interstate Parkway, take Exit 2, drive to the New Jersey Administration Office. Here a fine touring trail starts, first east, and then turns north. From 5 to 6 miles round trips, good for novices. Maps obtainable from New Jersey Administration Office, Box 155, Alpine, N.J. 07620. Tel. 201-

768-1360. New York City Office, 380 Madison Avenue, New York, N.Y. 10017. Tel. 212-JU 6-2440.

STOKES STATE FOREST, HIGH POINT STATE PARK.
FOR INTERMEDIATE SKIERS

The Appalachian Trail forms a backbone of this park, and many parts of the trail are suitable for touring, particularly because there is access to the trail from Route 203 and Route 23, which cross the park area. Within the park are several roads which are plowed in the winter. The smaller park roads, which are not plowed, make excellent ski-touring routes.

NEW YORK

ADIRONDACK MOUNTAINS

Most of the trails described below are suitable for novice skiers and have been selected to avoid any significant downgrades. In some cases, trails have been recommended where there are a few spots of local difficulty which are noted in the trail description. For those who have attained greater proficiency, the Adirondacks represent one of the last great wilderness areas to be found in the East and thus offer challenging opportunities for those seeking real winter adventure. In a few cases, trails requiring greater-than-novice proficiency have been mentioned and are so indicated. For some of the areas in the Adirondacks, the New York State Department of Environmental Conservation, Albany, N.Y. 12201, has a very detailed description and maps. They are listed as follows:

Eastern Adirondacks: Lake George; Crown Point Region (Knob Pond, Hammondsville, Over Shot Pond); Schroon Lake Region (Crane Pond, Putnam Pond, Pharaoh Lake, and the complex of trails that interconnects these places).

Northern Adirondacks: The Ausable Lakes; Keene Valley and the John Brook Trail; Lake Placid Region; Mount Van Hoevenberg Recreation Area; Adirondack Loj and the high peaks of Mount Marcy; Saranac Lake area horse trail to Fish Pond.

Central Adirondacks: The Northville Lake Placid Trail at Benson, Piesco, and Lake Durant; The Siamese Ponds; Gore Mountain.

Western Adirondacks: Thendara to Big Otter Lake.

Eastern Adirondacks

The Narrows of Lake George

The Narrows are one of the most scenic parts of Lake George, dotted with islands and prominent cliffs coming to the water's edge. Drive to Bolton Landing, and turn off on road to Green Island and Sagamore Hotel. Park near Norwall's boat livery, and follow side road left to lake and onto ice. Continue down the bay formed by Green Island and mainland; at tip of Green Island entire length of Tounge Mountain comes into view. Set a course slightly north of east to tip of Tounge Mountain. Once past this point you are in the Narrows and can thread your way in and out of the islands at will. From last week in January to early March, the lake is usually frozen solid and the hard wind-packed snow makes for fast touring.

Crown Point
Knob Pond–Hammond, a 7-Mile Round Trip

This tour starts from the Over Shot Area of North Ironville. The trail follows a gently rolling jeep trail to Knob Pond, covering a distance of 3½ miles.

Hammondsville

This tour departs from the Knob Pond trail and continues on to the old abandoned town of Hammondsville, a settlement during the early iron-ore mining days of the Crown Pond area. Here is a chance to see the remains of a ghost town and some of the once-used open-pit mines. Distance 7 miles round trip.

Over Shot Pond

Leaving the Hogback Road in North Ironville, the trail to Over Shot Pond follows a logging road for a distance of 8 miles into some of the most scenic parts of the eastern Adirondacks. This trip is most suitable for beginners.

Miller Mountain

Starting from the heart of Crown Point Village, the trail follows an old railroad bed, crosses meadows, and finally picks up an old logging road to the top of Miller Mountain and the Old Spar mines. Round trip is about 10 miles and is recommended for the more experienced ski tourers.

For further details on the above trails write Douglas Buckland, Box 223, Crown Point, N.Y. 12928.

Schroon Lake. The Crane Pond–Putnam Pond Region

This region is a compact wilderness area where a network of trails connect twenty-two small and large ponds. There are fourteen lean-tos dispersed in this area. The effects of past forest fires may be seen in bare snow slopes on some of the mountains. The country exhibits many cliffs and ledges which add to its scenic attractiveness, but as a consequence, many trails contain locally steep spots and these particular locations are not recommended for novice skiers.

Access to this area may be found: (1) from the west on the Crane Pond Road, (2) from the north via Route 73, and (3) from the east at Putnam Pond Public Campsite.

This area is shown on the Paradox Lake quadrangle, on U.S. topographic maps.

Interesting ski tours from the western side are: (1) Goose Pond, a secluded pond on a side trail set in a deep hemlock forest, (2) Crane Pond, (3) continuing past Crane Pond to the lower slopes of Pharaoh Mountain, (4) past the Pharaoh Mountain trail toward Pharaoh Lake, and (5) from the south via the village at Adirondack.

185

Western Approach

From the village of Schroon Lake, follow Route 9 north for 2 miles beyond the traffic light in Schroon Lake, and turn east (right) on the road marked for the ranger headquarters and for Crane Pond. Park cars at end of plowed road shortly after passing the ranger headquarters. The unplowed road continues to Crane Pond.

The trail to Goose Pond branches right from the unplowed road leading to Crane Pond, 1 mile from the start. The side trail to Goose Pond is .75 mile long, making this a very short, easy tour. Yellow markers.

Following the unplowed road, Crane Pond is reached in 2 miles. Cross the outlet of Crane Pond, and pick up the trail to Pharaoh Mountain, following red markers. The turnoff to the mountain itself is found about .75 mile beyond Crane Pond. The red markers go to the fire tower; the yellow markers continue to Pharaoh Lake. The lower reaches of the Pharaoh Mountain trail are suitable for skiing, but after about a mile, the trail becomes very steep and is not recommended.

Continuing on the yellow-marked trail toward Pharaoh Lake, a side trail branches left to Oxshoe Pond. This is very steep and not recommended. Another ski trail branches left 1.25 miles beyond the Pharaoh Mountain trail, to Crab Pond. This is skiable but quite steep. Experts only.

The Pharaoh Lake trail is recommended for about a mile or so beyond this last trail junction, at which point it begins a long and steep descent into Pharaoh Lake. Total distance from the beginning of this descent to the start of the unplowed road, 5 miles.

Approaches via Route 73. Trail to Tub Mill Marsh Lean-To, Lily Pad Pond, and Rock Pond

From Schroon Lake Village, take Route 9 north to the intersection of Route 73. This intersection nearly coincides with

Northway Exit 28. Drive east of Route 73 for 7.5 miles to the state signboard indicating the trail.

This trail has points of severe, local difficulty within .5 mile from the start. These may be bypassed by driving an additional .5 mile east on Route 73, where a body of water, right, indicates the outlet of Eagle Lake. A snowmobile trail passes across the dam at Eagle Lake outlet and continues back, crossing the hiking trail to Tub Mill Marsh lean-to in 1 mile. At this trail intersection, bear left, following blue markers. The trail drops into a small valley, then begins a gentle climb, crosses a low pass, then descends to Tub Mill Marsh lean-to. Distance to Route 73, 2 miles. Continuing on blue markers, Honey Pond is passed, left; then the trail reaches Lily Pad Pond and lean-to 3 miles from Route 73. Following blue markers farther leads to rough going and is not recommended.

Turning left (east) at Lily Pad Pond, a trail with red markers goes by easy grades to the northwestern end of Rock Pond. The trail continues completely around the lake, and Rock Pond lean-to is directly opposite.

From Rock Pond lean-to, the blue-marked trail continues south (or left when facing Rock Pond) and enters a forest so open as to permit glade skiing between the trees. Distance, Rock Pond lean-to to Route 73, 5 miles.

Routes Starting from
Putnam Pond Public Campsite

Driving directions: Campsite is reached by driving east on Route 73 for 12.5 miles from the Northway to the hamlet of Chilson. Turn right (south) on a road which dead-ends at the campsite. Park near the booth at the campsite entrance.

North from the Campsite to
Heart Pond and Bear Pond

This is essentially a level route suitable for novice skiers. Take any service road to the right when facing lake. These terminate in a loop at the extreme end of which the foot trail (yellow markers) leaves for Heart Pond and Bear Pond. Heart Pond is reached in slightly less than a mile. The trail forks here, the yellow markers leading around the northern side of North Pond to Rock Pond. This trail is narrow, with a number of steep pitches, and is intermediate to expert. Bear Pond is about 2 miles from the campsite.

Horse Trail from the Village of Adirondack to Pharaoh Lake

This medium-width bridle path has very easy grades for the first 4 miles. The next 2 miles contain severe locally steep spots. Distance to Pharaoh Lake, 6 miles.

Take the Northway to Pottersville. Leaving Pottersville north on Route 9, turn right .5 mile from Pottersville at the sign for the Word of Life camp. Follow a secondary road around the southern end of Schroon Lake for about 4 miles to the village of Adirondack.

At the general store in Adirondack, continue straight (due east) for .4 mile to a Y intersection. Take the left fork, and continue .2 mile to a T intersection; take left fork again. This road proceeds due north, and dead-ends in the parking lot at the head of the horse trail. The horse trail goes almost level, due north, for about 2 miles, then swings to the east and climbs slowly and steadily. In 4 miles it starts a precipitous descent into the valley of the Desolate Brook. This descent is the limit for ordinary ski touring; the remaining 2 miles to Pharaoh Lake are for experts.

NORTHERN ADIRONDACKS

The Ausable Lakes

The Ausable Lakes are two very narrow lakes set in a deep cleft in the mountains, with superb views. The area is approached by a carriage road and is suitable for novices who are in condition for a 7-mile round trip.

Driving directions: From Northway Exit 30 take Route 73 north for about 8 miles. After crossing a height of land the highway drops down a long, very steep hill. Just at the bottom of this hill turn left (west) at St. Huberts, an unidentified, small cluster of houses, and take a short, very steep road up that leads to the Ausable Club. Park cars at the club.

Please note: The entire route lies within the private park of the Adirondack Mountain Reserve. Summer and winter hikers are welcome with the provision that no fires are to be built and that there is to be no overnight camping. Carry out all lunch wrappers and picnic residue.

From the Ausable Club proceed down the hill to the gate at the start of the carriage road. Follow the road up gentle grades 3.5 miles to the foot of Lower Ausable Lake, which is 1.5 miles long. A short way up the lake notice the Fishhawk Cliffs, on the left, and a rock formation which bears resemblance to an Indian head.

Rainbow Falls

Cross the outlet of Lower Ausable Lake, and pick up a trail that follows the west shore of the lake. In about .25 mile there is a side trail to the right leading to the falls. The light on this striking waterfall, ice-sheathed in winter, is best in the morning.

Keene Valley: The John Brook Trail

This trail is the eastern approach to the ascent of Mount Marcy. The first 3.5 miles to John Brook Lodge (closed in winter) are wide, with a steady gentle upgrade that gains 1,000 feet in elevation. Beyond John Brook Lodge, the trail is narrower, with slightly steeper grades; Bushnell Falls, 5 miles from the start, represents the practical limit of this trail for ski touring. Beyond this point the trail becomes steep and is not recommended.

Take Route 73 to Keene Valley, and turn west at the main corner of the village at the signboard TRAILS TO MT. MARCY. Bear right at an iron bridge, and continue up a steep, winding

189

road to The Garden, a large open area 1.6 miles from Keene Valley. The trail departs from this point. Follow yellow trail markers.

Deer Brook lean-to is reached 1 mile from The Garden. Deer Brook ravine, just beyond, has steep sides and may require side-stepping descent under some snow conditions.

Lake Placid Region

This region in the Adirondacks has many opportunities for ski touring. Near Wilmington, the trail behind the Whiteface Chalet offers superb views of the entire area. To the south, the Mount Van Hoevenburg Recreation Area offers professionally laid-out and groomed ski-touring trails which interconnect with another complex of trails radiating from South Meadows and Adirondack Lodge. For the real expert are the trips over Klondike Notch, through Avalanche Pass into Lake Colden, and the winter ascent of Mount Marcy.

Bark Eater

Located near the famous Olympic Village of Lake Placid, this small, out-of-the-way touring center offers good ski touring. The specialty shop, established by two former Olympians, offers touring equipment for sale or rental. Instruction and guided tours are also available. In addition, the Bark Eater offers modest family-style accommodations in a comfortable old farmhouse. Gary Cogswell, Manager, Bark Eater Ski Touring Center, Alstead Mill Road, Keene, N.Y. 12942. Tel. 518-576-2221.

Mount Van Hoevenberg Recreation Area

This Nordic Ski Area is located just off the first parking lot at the Olympic Bob Run, 6 miles south of Lake Placid, off Route 73. The trails are in two connected sections at the foot of Mount Van Hoevenberg. The trails on the north side of the Bob Run

Road are designated as the North Meadow Loops, and those on the south side as Mount Van Hoevenberg Loops. There are ten loops, all starting and finishing at the same point. The trails, 12 miles in all, are designed for multipurpose use, ski touring, cross-country ski racing and training. There are short, easy loops for beginners and more difficult trails for the expert. There are no steep climbs or descents, all trails well marked as to degree of difficulty and with directional signs at junction points. These cross-country trails are maintained by members of the New York State Department of Conservation with special packing equipment. All trails are available for training purposes, as well as for races and ski touring. There is no charge for the use of these ski trails.

Connection Between the
Mount van Hoevenberg Trails and
Trails from Adirondack Loj

A connecting trail has been built between the Mount Van Hoevenberg trail complex and South Meadows. South Meadows is the connection point for the Mount Van trail to Adirondack Loj, the Truck Trail to Marcy Dam, the Klondike Trail to the Klondike Pass, and the road to Route 93. This connection trail leaves the Mount Van Hoevenberg area at High Notch, the eastern end of Mount Hoevenberg. There is a steep descent at the top, soon becoming gradual. A lean-to is reached in about 1 mile at the crossing of South Meadow Brook. Two miles from High Notch, it joins the trail from South Meadows to the Klondike. Turn right at this trail junction. In 600 feet, the trail forks, the right fork goes directly to South Meadows, and the road about .5 mile distant. The left fork crosses the Marcy Dam Fire Truck Trail in about .5 mile and continues as the Mount Van trail to Adirondack Loj.

Adirondack Loj. Box 867, Lake Placid 12946.
9 Miles South of Lake Placid. 518-523-3441

Probably the most extensive system of ski-touring trails in the eastern United States radiates from Adirondack Loj and Heart Lake in the Adirondack Mountains of northern New York state. A ski-touring trail and motor road connect the Loj trails to the 12-mile ski-touring and racing-trail complex maintained by the State of New York—the Mount Van Hoevenberg Recreation Area. (See description of Van Hoevenberg area on page 190.) In addition, there are many miles of touring on world-famed Lake Placid Lake, with its dramatic mountain setting, on fire-truck trails and other skiable mountain trails in the vicinity. Adirondack Loj, dating back to 1880, is at the very base of the Adirondack High Peak Area, now a modern building operated by the Adirondack Mountain Club, with dining room, bunk-rooms, and some private rooms. Equipment for rental and sale, touring lessons upon prior arrangements.

Trails from Heart Lake and Adirondack Loj

A round trip of 4.5 miles to Rocky Falls lean-to, 8 miles round trip to Scott Clearing and lean-to. Beautiful forest, rolling terrain, intermediate. Red markers. Leaving the main building of Adirondack Loj and skirting under the flank of Mount Jo, the trail goes around the north shore of Heart Lake. (With suitable conditions the lake may be traversed.) The first climb occurs just beyond the lake, after which the grades are very easy to another climb at Rocky Falls. Just over 2 miles from the Loj, a side trail marked LEAN-TO leads to Indian Pass Brook and Rocky Falls lean-to. After a small rise the main trail continues to Scott Clearing lumber-camp area at a moderate grade. The very steep ascent into Indian Pass starts just ahead and is not suitable for ski touring.

Wright Peak Ski Mountaineering Trail

A round trip of 5 miles, more than 2,000-foot climb. Lower part easy grade, middle section moderate, top steep and narrow. This is a mountain touring trail. Get directions and advice at Loj. Suitable for expert and advanced intermediate skiers—start

192

on the hiking trail from Adirondack Loj to Marcy Dam (sign trailside register here). Turn right at the sign indicating MacIntyre–Algonquin Peak. One-half mile farther, on the Algonquin Trail, a fairly wide branch to the left crosses MacIntyre Brook, and there is a weathered sign on the opposite bank: WRIGHT PEAK. Bear right after .25 mile, where the Whale's Tail Trail branches left. The last .25 mile to the actual summit is not maintained as a ski trail.

Whale's Trail

Suitable for intermediate skiers. In combination with the Marcy Dam hiking trail, the Whale's Tail forms a loop between Adirondack Loj and Marcy Dam. It climbs through the pass between Whale's Tail Mountain and Wright Peak, starting near the beginning of the Wright Peak Trail. For approach from Loj see description of Wright Peak. Dropping into Marcy Dam after a 500-foot climb, the loop totals about 5 miles.

Marcy Dam Trail

Sometimes called the Loj Trail, this is a must for fairly competent skiers. Blue markers. Some short, moderately steep pitches and rolling terrain through pleasant woods for 2.2 miles round trip to Marcy Dam where there are several lean-tos and fireplaces.

About 1.75 miles from Adirondack Loj, the ski trail leaves the hiking trail by going through the woods to the east a short distance, crosses Marcy Brook, and picks up the Fire Trail, which is directly opposite.

Marcy Dam Fire Trail

About 7 miles round trip from Adirondack Loj to Marcy Dam on the gentle grades of Mount Van Trail connecting with the unplowed truck trail. Start at the Loj gate opposite the sign DEAD END ROAD. This trail is the beginning of the Mount Van Trail which connects Adirondack Loj with the Mount Van

Hoevenberg cross-country trails. It goes through deep spruce woods, then enters an open area with a gentle downhill slide. Cross Marcy Brook and an open meadow with a beautiful view of the mountains. Just beyond, note pond to the left which contains a large beaver house. At the junction with the state truck trail 1.5 miles from the Loj, turn right for easy going about 2 miles to Marcy Dam. This is the best novice route from Adirondack Loj to Marcy Dam. For variety, over slightly more difficult terrain, a loop may be completed back to the Loj by the Whale's Tail or Loj hiking trail.

An enjoyable trip to Marcy Dam on the Marcy Dam Fire Trail may be had by starting from South Meadows (see below). At the end of the South Meadows road, turn right, pass a motor vehicle barrier, and cross a bridge over South Meadows Brook. This is the start of the Fire Trail. About .5 mile up the Fire Trail look for the Mount Van Trail from Adirondack Loj, approaching from the right, and the continuation of this trail to Mount Van Hoevenberg—left.

Mount Marcy

New York's highest mountain (5,344 feet) is 14 miles round trip and more than 3,000 feet above Adirondack Loj. The summit is about 500 feet above timberline. This is ski mountaineering for experts only. From Marcy Dam (see Marcy Dam Trail, above) take the blue Mount Marcy Trail. At junctions follow specifically cut trail (wider than hiking trails). Look for "Ski" markers. Indian Falls is about 2 miles from Marcy Dam. For a tremendous view of the MacIntyre Range, go downstream from main trails a few yards to head of falls. Indian Falls, at about 3700 feet, is a good trip in itself. There are two lean-tos here and two more about 1.5 miles beyond, near timberline. *Take note—Warning:* Trail above last lean-to may be completely snowed under. Do not go above timberline under conditions of poor visibility or high wind, as tracks drift in and disappear. Temperature and wind chill can become extreme. Considered a hazardous location. Get directions and advice at

Loj. This ascent is only for experts with winter mountaineering experience! Be sure to sign trailside registers at Loj and Marcy Dam.

Avalanche Pass to Tahawus Village

This 10-mile trail from Adirondack Loj to Tahawus bisects the high peak wilderness. A 4-mile, 700-foot climb, some of it very steep, leads to three lakes in Avalanche Pass. Yellow trail from Marcy Dam to Lake Colden. Return by same route from the pass to Avalanche lean-tos is difficult because of steep, narrow trail unofficially known as Misery Hill. Watch out for telephone wire, which hangs low in deep snow. With high cliffs on each side, Avalanche Pass has some of the finest mountain scenery in the East. A ranger's cabin (occupied) is approximately halfway to Tahawus, on Lake Colden.

Saranac Lake. Horse Trail to Fish Pond

This medium-width bridle path is generally level, with the exception of one climb 3.5 miles from the start. It goes 5.5 miles to Fish Pond, where there is a lean-to. From Saranac Lake, take Route 86 to Lake Clear Junction. Continue on Route 86 to the intersection of a side road, left, leading back to Saranac Lake. At this point, note the Conservation Department's headquarters on the right, where parking is available.

The trail leaves as a road just beyond the headquarters. Cross the old railroad bed and turn left, following the railroad for about .25 mile. The horse trail turns right away from the railroad and enters the woods to Fish Pond.

CENTRAL ADIRONDACKS

The Northville–Lake Placid Trail

This famous wilderness hiking trail generally follows the valleys and much of it is suitable for ski touring. Between road crossings there may be unbroken wilderness stretches of 25 to 50 miles.

Those parts of the trail suitable for ski touring within the limits of a 12-mile round trip are given below.

Northville–Lake Placid Trail, Benson to Silver Lake Lean-to

This is an excellent route on old logging roads. The route proceeds with a gentle climb affording an almost continuous run back. Distance to Silver Lake, 7 miles one way. Rock Lake, 4 miles one way, is another objective.

From the New York State Thruway, exit at Amsterdam; take Route 30 north. Watch for the bridge across the head of Sacandaga Reservoir at Northville, and 3.2 miles beyond, turn left on road to Benson. Follow this side road 2.9 miles after crossing iron bridge, turn right on dirt road, continue north through Benson Center. Road swings left, follow to end of plowed road.

Northville–Lake Placid Trail, Piseco South to Hamilton Stream Lean-to

On Route 8 at Piseco Central School, locate trail signboard and proceed south across open field. Where trail enters woods look for blue trail markers. There is a false trail, to the left, that also leaves this field.

The trail is on a slight upgrade to a height of land, then descends more or less continuously. Hamilton Stream lean-to is 3.6 miles on the left side of the trail.

North from Piseco

At Piseco Central School, turn on a side road leading to the village of Piseco. In about 2 miles, turn right at a sign for Haskells Hotel. The road dead-ends in a parking lot at the start of the trail.

The trail proceeds due north for about 2 miles on the level, swings left, descends briefly, then ascends a wet-weather stream bed. There may be washouts of the snow here after a thaw. After this climb the trail continues through open forest to the crossing

196

of Fall Stream, 5 miles from the start. Beyond this point, there is about 35 miles of wilderness travel to the next plowed road.

South to Stephens Pond

At the ranger headquarters, follow the service roads around the eastern end of Lake Durant. In .3 mile, the trail branches left. Look for blue trail markers. The trail starts an upgrade at this point. There is a moderately steep section 1 mile in. At the top of this rise, and 1.6 miles from the start, look for a tree with a red-painted blaze. At this point, leave the trail, and proceed directly through the forest to Stephens Pond .25 mile away. This detour will save a climb and a steep descent to Stephens Pond lean-to, located on the southwestern edge of the lake near the far end.

From Lake Durant Public Campsite

The Northville Placid Trail crosses Route 28 between Indian Lake and Blue Mountain Lake at the Lake Durant Public Campsite.

North from Lake Durant to Tirrell Pond

From ranger headquarters, go about 1,000 feet west on Route 28. The trail enters the woods at the top of a highway cut.

One mile from the highway the trail enters the lands of a private paper company. This area may contain newly cut roads for lumbering operations. Follow blue trail markers carefully for the next 1.5 miles. The trail now reenters state lands. A little more than 3 miles from the road is the first Tirrell Pond lean-to. The trail goes up the west side of the pond for 1 mile to the second lean-to at the north end of the pond. Beyond this point, the trail enters lumbered lands and, beyond this, encounters cliffs.

North Creek Region–the Siamese Ponds

The Siamese Ponds offer a 14-mile round trip through prime wilderness country, following the east branch of the Sacandaga

River part of the way. With the exception of one sharp climb at the outset, the route is generally level.

The trail starts out over a shoulder of Eleventh Mountain. The height of land is reached in .5 mile, and the confluence of Diamond Brook and the Sacandaga River is reached in 1.5 miles. In 3 miles the trail forks; take the left fork to the Siamese Ponds, 4 more miles distant.

From the Adirondack Northway exit at Warrensburg, take Route 9 through Warrensburg, and turn left on Route 28 to Wevertown and North Creek. At Wevertown take Route 8, left, and drive about 10 miles through Johnsburg, Sodom, and Bakers Mills. The trail starts 4 miles beyond Bakers Mills on the right-hand (north) side of Route 8. White farmhouse (Harrington's) is about .25 mile from the trail going toward Bakers Mills.

Rum Runner

Located at the Alp Horn Inn, the Rum Runner offers a complete facility for ski touring. The equipment and accessories are available from the Nordic specialty shop. Also available are an excellent trail system, instruction, guided tours, lunches, a lounge, and accommodations in the Gore Mountain area. Pelle Axblad, Manager, Rum Runner Ski Touring Center, Alp Horn Inn, Loon Lake, N.Y. 12951. Tel. 518-494-3811.

WESTERN ADIRONDACKS

Old Forge Region

The unplowed state truck trails from Thendara permit interesting touring for all skiers. Take Route 12 from Utica, then No. 28 to Thendara and look for Conservation Department sign TRAIL TO MOOSE RIVER MT., just before the overhead railroad bridge. Park at the end of the plowed road leading toward Moose River Mountain. For details write to Conservation Department for *Winter Hiking in the New York State Forest Reserve*. Maps available. For information contact Bob Hall,

Tourist Information Center, Old Forge, N.Y. 13420. Tel. 315-369-6983.

NEAR THE CAPITAL DISTRICT, NEW YORK

Schenectady Municipal Golf Course,
off Oregon Road, Schenectady

Albany Municipal Golf Course, New Scotland Avenue, Albany

Ski touring on golf courses is usually best on the edges of the fairways at the edge of the woods. The snow tends to be wind-blown in the middle of the open areas. All winter users of golf courses should avoid the putting greens.

Glens Falls: Night-lighted Cross-country Ski Trails.
Crandall Park

Crandall Park is located on Route 9 on the north end of Glens Falls. One of the few lighted ski-touring facilities to permit night skiing in the United States at this time.

J. B. Thacher State Park. Located on New York Route 157,
18 Miles Southwest of Albany

Developed ski-touring trails for beginners and novices are available at the Hop Field Picnic Area, where parking and a winterized comfort station is available.

There are three trail loops, varying in length from .25 mile to nearly 1.5 miles.

Open-slope and cross-country skiing is also available on parklands south of the Beaver Dam Road, where a parking area is maintained. Skiers must walk up the slope at this location since mechanical tows are not available.

Moreau Lake State Park. Located off U.S. Route 9,
South Glens Falls, on Old Saratoga Road, just South of
Interstate 87, Exit 17-S

Ski touring may be enjoyed on footpaths along west shore of

199

the lake, through the picnic areas, along the park nature trail, and over other trails. Limited parking and a winterized comfort station are available in the transient camping loop.

Patridge Run Wildlife Management Area

This 4,500-acre area contains 21 miles of newly cut trails, in combination with mowed open areas and a number of small ponds, all on rolling, upland plateau about 25 miles southwest of Albany. Elevation 1,800 to 2,000 feet.

The unplowed roads in this same area are used by snowmobiles, but the trails are open to all public use except by motorized vehicles. The trails are distinguished by a small parking lot together with a sturdy pipe barrier. Most of these start from roads not plowed in winter. Skiers are cautioned to carry a compass and to take note of all intersections, as the web of look-alike trails and open areas can be confusing.

The village of Berne is at the intersection of Routes 43 and 146, about 25 miles southwest of Albany. Starting at Berne Central School and heading west, take a Y fork off Route 43. Follow this road for .5 mile and turn right on Sickle Hill Road. Sickle Hill Road crosses a creek, then proceeds up a hill of increasing steepness, becoming one of the steepest roads in New York at a set of hairpin turns. *Caution here.* About 2.5 miles from the start, note a ruined wooden church on the right, and .2 mile beyond, park at an unplowed road leading right. Ski down road .25 mile, and turn right at a barrier on a side trail. This is one entrance to the trail network, and many branching trails will be found farther in.

This area administered by the Bureau of Fish and Wildlife, New York State Department of Environmental Conservation, Stamford, N.Y.

Grafton Lake State Park. Located off New York Route 2, 10 Miles East of Troy

Ski-touring opportunities are available through woodlands

and on footpaths and roads in the bathhouse-picnic area complex at the south end of Long Lake and around Shaver Lake. Limited parking is available near the park maintenance center on Long Pond Road. For a bulletin giving a complete listing of many ski-touring facilities convenient to the capital district, write Eastern New York Ski Touring Association, PO Box 145, Rotterdam Junction, N.Y. 12150.

Saratoga National and Historic Park

The site of the Saratoga battlefield of Revolutionary War fame is now preserved as a national park. Many miles of unplowed park roads and open fields. Separate areas for ski touring and snowmobiles. Park entrance buildings open and heated in winter. Highly recommended.

From Albany, take U.S. Route 4 to Stillwater, N.Y., then take Route 32 to the park entrance.

Burnt Hills, N.Y., The Fo'castle Farms ski touring is welcome through an extensive and well-kept apple orchard and adjoining farm property. There is a snack bar on the premises. The village of Burnt Hills is off Route 50 between Schenectady and Ballston Spa. Ski-touring instruction and rentals available.

Rensselaerville. The Cheese Hill Reforestation Area

This area is about 25 miles southwest of Albany, at an elevation of 2,000 feet, with excellent snow conditions. There are no marked ski trails as such in this area, but there are open pine glades, fields with extensive views of the Catskill forest lanes, and state truck trails usually unplowed in winter.

Take Route 85 to Rensselaerville. Turn right in the village and follow signs to the Edward P. Cass Youth Camp, about 2 miles distant. The youth-camp grounds themselves are restricted, so park at Cheese Hill Road, just beyond. Go up the hill, and follow a lane that parallels Cheese Hill Road to the start of the truck trail about .5 mile distant. Many side trips to explore the area are possible from the truck trail.

201

FINGER LAKES REGION

Trumansburg
Podunk Trails Along Taughannock Creek

Marked trails from 1 to 4 kilometers, suitable for novice and intermediate skiers. Trails also for those who wish to train for cross-country racing. Ski programs for children.

Call for details: Osmo O. Heila, 607-387-6716. Podunk Cross-Country Ski Shop, RD 1, Podunk Road.

A bulletin giving complete ski-touring information in the Finger Lakes region has been prepared by the Cornell University Outing Club, Willard Straight Hall, Cornell University, Ithaca, N.Y. 14850, or care of K. P. Parkinson, 229 North Triphammer Road, Ithaca, N.Y. 14850.

Connecticut Hill Wildlife Management Area.
13 Miles South of Ithaca

Fourteen miles of blazed trail partially on unplowed roads, but mostly on wooded paths. The three access points are described on the back of clearly printed trail maps available (free) at Ithaca area ski shops. Maps show degree of difficulty for various sections of the trail. Deer and wild turkey are often seen along the way.

Greek Peak Touring Ski Trails—Virgil.
10 Miles South of Cortland

Fifteen miles of unplowed roads make good ski touring behind the famous central New York alpine ski area. Short (3.6 miles), intermediate (5.6 miles), and long (8.9 miles) loop trails are shown on maps available (free) at Ithaca area ski shops. (Maps not available at Greek Peak.) The best access point to these unblazed trails is described on the map. Snow in the Virgil area permits some of the earliest and latest ski touring of the season in central New York.

Hammond Hill—Caroline.
15 Miles Southeast of Ithaca

Seven-mile ski-touring loop on unplowed roads. Bring a compass and one of the ski-touring maps of the area. Notes on the map minimize the possibilities of wrong turns. Maps for this unblazed trip are available (free) at Ithaca area ski shops. Excellent hilltop views of the rolling terrain in central New York can be seen from several high points on this trip.

CATSKILL MOUNTAINS

Haines Falls Horse Trails.
Near North Lake Public Campsite

A complex of old carriage roads used in the nineteenth century makes fine twentieth-century ski-touring trails. Some of these are now marked as horse trails. At places, these trails approach a line of cliffs which rim the entire area, affording spectacular views of the Hudson River. *Warning:* Approach the edge of the escarpment with great caution in winter, because of the possibility of white ice lightly covered with snow. This is likely to form on slopes facing south. Stay on the horse trails, and avoid the blue-marked summer Escarpment Trail, which runs directly above the line of cliffs.

Take Route 23-A to Haines Falls, and turn north in the village on the road leading to North Lake Public Campsite. At a distance of 2.2 miles from the village, turn right on a side road marked with a Conservation Department sign indicating Kaaterskill Falls. The road terminates in a parking lot in 1 mile. The Escarpment Trail leaves right from the parking lot (avoid!); the horse-trail complex departs left behind the barrier.

Directly behind the barrier the trail forks. The left fork, unmarked, goes to South Lake, then North Lake. The site of the historic Mountain House with spectacular views lies about .5 mile southeast of this point. Total distance 1.5 miles.

The right fork, red markers, reaches the site of the old Kaaterskill House in 1.5 miles. Continuing straight ahead on blue markers, Boulder Rock, with sweeping views, is reached 2.5 miles from the start.

Belleayre Ski Center, Highmont

This area provides a large choice of trails, suitable for novice, intermediate, and expert. Short trips of a few miles or all-day tours can be planned. All trails are wide and well kept; many are rated for novices to intermediate skiers, but experts also have a choice of runs. Those wishing to avoid too much climbing may use the Belleayre or Highmount ski lifts.

Following are a few sample trails: (1) Start from lodge at top of Belleayre upper chair lift, go along Ridge Trail to Highmount Ski Area, and return via Deer Run Trail; distance about 2 miles. (2) From Belleayre Base Lodge ski up Roaring Brook Trail and along Ridge Trail to Fire Tower about 1.5 miles: from here you may return to lodge, or ski down Fire Trail to Pine Hill; this last section is for intermediate skiers only.

Hunter Mountain Area

Suitable for novice and intermediate skiers, top part for experts. Distance about 6.25 miles on lower part. Top part 2.5 miles. Enter at Spruceton. A very gentle climb over unplowed road and CCC road to the Col, about 3.5 miles with 1,000 feet climbing. This part is suitable for novices and offers an easy downhill run through the woods. Roads need only 8 inches of snow.

From the Col, the trail rises sharply to the Rob Shelter in .5 mile and then reaches the summit of Hunter in 1.5 miles. Total climbing from the Col, 1,100 feet. The section from the Col to the shelter is for experienced skiers only.

Lake Minnewaska

Six touring trails available. Novice to expert, varying from 2 to 12 miles, maps posted in lobby of Wildmere House, ask for Mr. Erbe. Take New York Thruway Exit 18, west of Route 299. Then 5 miles on Route 44 to entrance Lake Minnewaska.

Novice Trail No. 1

Around Lake Minnewaska. Distance 2 miles. Trip takes 1 to 1½ hours. Coming from main lobby of Wildmere House, turn right. Views of Lake Minnewaska on right. Proceed on same path and go over pass which joins path again to Cliff House. Proceed up to Cliff House. Follow path around back of water tower and on your right until hotel is reached.

Novice Trail No. 2

Beacon Hill and return. Distance 3 miles. Two-hour trip. Coming from main lobby of Wildmere House, turn right. Proceed down main entrance road to road to Lake Minnewaska Estate. Take first path past garage entrance (there is no sign marking Beacon Hill path). Stay on this path until end. Excellent view from Beacon Hill. Return via same route.

Intermediate Trail No. 3

Castle Point and return. Distance 8 miles. Four-hour trip. Coming from main lobby of Wildmere House, turn left and around hotel, and descend to lake level. Follow trail up marked CASTLE POINT, keeping left (golf course will be on your right), leaving lake on left (green will appear shortly on right). Path will proceed in southerly direction. Kampton Ledge will appear on your left. Ledge will be on your left all the way to Castle Point. Return on same route.

Intermediate Trail No. 4

Millbrook Mountain and return. Distance 8 miles. Four-hour trip. Coming from main lobby of Wildmere House, turn left and around hotel and descend to lake level. Follow trail up marked CASTLE POINT, keeping left (golf course will be on your right). Continue on trail marked LAKE SHORE DRIVE, keeping lake to your left. Turn off Lake Shore Drive on path marked GERTRUDE'S NOSE. Excellent views of Wallkill and Hudson valleys. Return via same route.

Expert Trail No. 5

Ski Minne via Awosting Falls. Distance 8 miles. Trip takes 5 to 6 hours. From main lobby of Wildmere House, turn left and around hotel. Proceed down path, but do not go down to lake level. Rather, take first path to right (not marked). Proceed on this path (hotel will be on your right), descending on winding trail to main entrance road of Lake Minnewaska Estate. Go down this road for 100 feet and take first path to right. Stay on this descending path, again making right turn as path joins main road. Awosting Falls on left. Stay on the descending path to bottom of falls, and continue on path with Peter's Hill on left. As path approaches U.S. Route 44, take path right. Trail parallels Route 44. Continue on until overhead bridge. Take paved road left, and Ski Minne will appear on right shortly. Food available at Ski Minne. Return via same route. Note: This trip has a 600-foot drop from Lake Minnewaska.

Expert Trail No. 6

Awosting Lake via Castle Point. Distance 12 miles. Trip takes 6 to 7 hours. Follow directions of Trail No. 3 to Castle Point. Continue on same path, gradually descending from Castle Point. Lake Awosting will appear below on left. Keep on path marked HOTELS (do not take trails on left). Fine view of Lake Awosting will appear on left. Keep on trail marked HOTELS, which generally bears right. At Lake Minnewaska turn left and ascend to hotel. Note: Be sure to take a trail lunch on trip.

Lake Mohonk Area

Mohonk Lake, New Paltz, N.Y. 12561. Tel. 914-255-1000. Direct New York City dialing, 233-2244. Ninety minutes on the Thruway (Exit 18) from New York City. Approximately 65 miles of groomed touring trails that wind through 7,500 acres comprising the Mohonk Mountain House and Mohonk Trust properties. The majority of the touring trails are situated on carriage paths that are used in the summer by horse-drawn carriages and walkers. After each snow, a snowmobile with track setter packs out trails. (This is the only snowmobile allowed on the properties.) The trails at Mohonk are for the novice and intermediate skier. A season skiing pass can be purchased which allows access to both Mohonk and Mohonk Trust lands at various points of entry. Maps of trails and roads can be obtained at the Mohonk gatehouse or by writing to the above address. There is a rental shop in the hotel where equipment can be obtained. Accommodations, instructions, and tours are available at the hotel.

Mount Tremper Area

Suitable for experienced skiers only. Distance 5 miles. The trail starts on Route 28 about .5 mile southeast of Phoenicia and follows a jeep road 2.75 miles to the top (shelter).

Phoenicia. On Route 28, Scandinavia Ski Village

A fully equipped cross-country ski-touring center with a variety of trails and cross-country ski school, with 2-, 3-, 5-, and 7-mile cross-country trails for beginners, intermediates, and advanced ski tourers.

The cross-country center includes the 20,000-square-foot log ski shop. Restaurant and motel. Equipment for sale and rent.

Rosendale. Williams Lake

Ski-touring trails and racing trails are measured, marked, and maintained by the Rosendale Nordic Ski Club. Besides the 6 miles of maintained trails, there are old logging roads that can be used by the tourer. All trails start at and loop back to Williams Lake Hotel. A rental and sales shop for Nordic touring equipment is on the premises. Beginners are urged not to try the cross-country racing trails. The beginnings of trails are marked accordingly.

Slide Mountain Area—Slide Mountain

Suitable for experienced skiers only. Distance 7 miles. Trail starts at Winnisook Lodge and climbs 1,700 feet in 3.5 miles to the summit. The trail is wide enough to provide pleasant skiing, provided no lumbering operations are in progress.

Winnisook Lodge to Fox Hollow

Suitable for experienced skiers only. Distance 9 miles. Traverse from Winnisook Lodge to Fox Hollow, over the Giant Ledges and Panther Mountain. While this is not a ski trail, it affords a splendid trip for hardy and experienced skiers. Length 9 miles with about 1,700 feet of climbing. Depending on snow conditions, the trip, never an easy one under the best of conditions, may offer a real challenge to the ski mountaineer.

NEW YORK CITY VICINITY

Bear Mountain

A trail approximately 3 miles, The Doddletown Ski Trail, a loop starting at parking lot near ice-skating rink.

Harriman Section

Ski trail in back of Silvermine Ski area. You can reach this from the Silvermine parking lot. There are several steep grades and turns.

Park at Lake Sebago in area used by fishermen. Carry skis across 7 Lakes Parkway. Ski east toward Pine Meadow Lake. There is a fine dirt road used in summer by fishermen. Ski north and west on dirt road back to paved road (7 Lakes Parkway). You will come out about 1 mile north of the Sebago parking area.

Rockland Lake North Area

Park in Number 2 parking lot at Rockland Lake North area. Carry skis easterly on Lake Road; at intersection turn left (easterly) and walk to bottom of hill where paved road turns south. Ski south from gate to Nyack Beach. This dirt road provides excellent skiing parallel to the Hudson River. Return must be over the same road to Rockland Lake North.

Maps available from Palisades Interstate Park Commission, Bear Mountain State Park, N.Y. 10911. Tel. Stony Point 6-2701.

Ward Pound Ridge Reservation
Within About One-Hour Drive from Manhattan

There are 4,500 acres of hilly woodlands with a new 8-foot-wide trail for ski touring. Elevation from 300 feet to 860 feet. Most of the trails are so clean and smooth that a few inches of snow make them ready for ski touring. Trials are marked especially for skiing. The best way to select a trip is to study the U.S. Geological Survey topographic maps, the Pound Ridge Quadrangle, for the southern end of the reservation, and the Peach Lake Quadrangle for the northern end.

Ski-touring trips are possible in distances from 2 to 3 miles up to 20 miles with great variety in the terrain. Novices, intermediate, and expert.

Entrances to parking are at northern end of reservation located at Cross River at the intersection of Route 35 and Route 121. A small downhill skiing (and sleigh or toboggan riding) slope is right by the parking area. Open-air shelters available for picnics.

From Manhattan take Saw Mill River Parkway to end at Katonah. Follow Route 35 east to Cross River, south a few hundred feet to the entrance road to reservation. For information on snow conditions, call 914-SO 3-3184, Bjorn Kjellstrom, Fridays only, between 6 and 8 P.M.

New York State Additional

Snow Ridge, Turin

Tug Hill Touring Trail at Snow Ridge is suitable for intermediate skiers. Length is about 3 miles. Starts at top of Snow Pocket T-bar lift, crosses level fields and open country, winds through timberland, returns to ski area via an old-time settlers' road through a scenic gorge. Conducted tours are scheduled for this trail, leaving Snow Ridge Chalet at 2 P.M. on Sunday afternoons, conducted by the Snow Ridge Ski Patrol. Tel. 315-348-8644. Write Snow Ridge, Turin, N.Y. 13473.

Near Syracuse

LaFayette—Erie Bridge Ski Center

Take LaFayette exit off Interstate 81, west on Route 20 to Tully Farms Road, then south to first crossroad (Otisco Road). Or take Tully Exit off Interstate 81, then west to Tully Farms Road, then north to Otisco Road. Beginning and intermediate trails. Historic Erie Canal Bridge on one trail and warming shack offer more local color of that era. Ski shop, warming room, instructions and rentals. Erie Bridge Ski Center, PO Box 65, LaFayette, N.Y. Tel. 315-677-3637.

Tully, near Syracuse "Hill & Dale," 2 miles east of Tully Exit 81, proceed to traffic light, continue 2 miles ahead to Hill & Dale. The trail complex offers a 1.2-mile beginner trail that is lighted for night touring; a 2.4-mile trail serves intermediate tourers. Trails up to 9 miles in length are available for advanced tourers and cross-country racers. The Hill & Dale clubhouse features dining facilities, cocktail lounge, equipment for sale and rent. Group tours available weekends. Instructions daily including evenings.

Wing Hollow

Wing Hollow Ski Touring Center is located in the heart of some of the most beautiful rolling terrain western New York has to offer. Conveniently located for people in the Rochester, Buffalo, and Cleveland areas. Nordic specialty shop offers equipment and accessories, ski rentals, instruction, and guided tours. Refreshments available at the nearby Glass Works. James Kolocotronis, Manager, Wing Hollow Ski Touring Center, Ski Wing Ski Resort, Allegany, N.Y. 14706. Tel. 716-372-9130.

NEW YORK PARKS AND RECREATION AREAS OFFERING SKI TOURING

The length of the trails in the parks varies from a mile to several miles. They make use of walkways, hiking trails, nature trails, and unplowed roads and are separate from snowmobile trails. In some of the parks, as in John Boyd Thacher State Park, a plowed parking field and a convenient, heated comfort building form the starting point of the trails. In others with little winter usage, there are no particular facilities provided other than parking space. Brochures with further details can be obtained from the State of New York Parks and Recreation, Albany, N.Y. 12226, Alexander Aldrich, Commissioner, or from the following state parks:

Allegany—Route 17, 7 miles west of Salamanca.
Grafton Lakes—Route 2, 12 miles east of Troy.
John Boyd Thacher—Route 157, off Route 85, 15 miles southwest of Albany.

Moreau Lake—Exit 17-S off Route 87 (Northway) south of Glens Falls.

Thompson's Lake Camping Area—Route 157, 3 miles southwest of Thacher.

Green Lakes—10 miles east of Syracuse, Routes 290 and 5.

Cayuga Lake—3 miles east of Seneca Falls, Route 89.

Robert H. Treman—5 miles southwest of Ithaca, Route 13.

Fillmore Glen—1 mile south of Moravia, Route 38.

Bear Mountain—45 miles north of New York City, Palisades Interstate Parkway.

Harriman—35 miles north of New York City, Palisades Interstate Parkway.

Rockland Lake—18 miles north of New York City, U.S. Route 9-W.

Higley Flow—Coldbrook Drive off Route 56, 1.5 miles west of South Colton.

Jacques Cartier—2 miles south of Morristown River Road.

Robert Moses—2 miles north of Route 87, east of Massena.

Wellesley Island—2 miles north of Thousand Islands Bridge.

Saratoga Spa—Exit 13-N of Northway, Route 87.

ADDITIONAL TRAILS AS REPORTED BY THE TRAVEL BUREAU OF THE NEW YORK STATE DEPARTMENT OF COMMERCE

Big Tupper (Tupper Lake)—Many forest and logging trails and roads in the immediate area.

Mohonk (New Paltz)—Bonticou Touring Trail. Five miles. Piney Woods Touring Trail, 6 miles.

Peek'n Peak (French Creek)—About 1.5 to 2 miles in length, a mixture of cross-country and easy downhill from top of lift back to base lodge.

Greek Peak (Cortland)—Six-mile cross-country.

Ander-Lan (Little York)—Grandma's Trail, .8 mile, partly through woods.

Drumlins—Cross-country trail, 3 miles.

West Mountain—Twenty-four miles of touring trails on top of the mountain lead to excellent views.

Swain—Mark Heath Cross-country Trail, 1 mile.

Central-Western Area—Bristol Mountain (Canandaigua); Cockaigne (Cherry Creek); Frost Ridge (LeRoy); Mount Otsego (Cooperstown); Song Mountain (Tully); Big Basin Ski Area (Allegany State Park); Addison Pinnacle (Addison).

Southern Area—Bald Hill Ski Bowl (Farmingville); Bethpage (Farmingdale); Grossinger Ski Bowl (Grossinger); Homestead (Pattersonville); Kutsher's Country Club (Monticello); Hillside Inn (Narrowsburg); Rocking Horse Ranch (Highland); Ski Minne (New Paltz); Snow Valley (Fishkill); Williams Lake Hotel (Rosendale).

Northern Area—Dynamite Hill (Chestertown); Mount Pisgah (Saranac Lake); Maple Ridge (Old Forge); McCauley Mountain (Old Forge); Royal Mountain (Johnstown); Seven Springs Sports Center (Colton).

Snow Ridge, Turin—George Trail, novice and intermediate, 2.5 miles, 500-foot vertical drop. On Route 12-D, trail starts near upper terminal of double chair. Trails packed.

Syracuse—Good trails on Drumlins Golf Course, in Heiberg Memorial Forest and Green Lakes State Forest.

PENNSYLVANIA

BLACK FOREST SKI TOURING TRAIL

Starting point: Thirty-two miles north of Jersey Shore, on Route 44-N, and 40 miles from Coudersport, on Route 44-S.

Trail: A 7-mile loop trail returning to starting point.

Markers: Light-blue 3-inch enamel dots, blazed on trees facing each direction; double blazes at all turns or abrupt direction changes.

The trail starts across Route 44 from a small parking area and enters a pine forest in a northwesterly direction for 100 yards.

Trail turns right in a northerly direction through a mixed forest of pine, young spruce, and oak on a level terrain for .5 mile. Trail enters basin at head of Spruce Hollow, and half-circles hollow head in a northwesterly direction. Trail intersects orange-dotted Black Forest Hiking Trail. Ski trail now follows hiking trail for 4 miles. Blue dots are beneath orange dots on trees.

Trail climbs for 100 yards to top of mountain plateau and enters a vast, flat forested area. Level terrain ski touring at its best—no underbrush. Oak forest with scattered maple and white birch. Trail intersects Refuge Trail and follows it in westerly direction for 1 mile near edge of mountain, providing scenic vistas at two points, overlooking Baldwin Branch of Young Womans Creek.

Trail enters northern hardwood forest for .75 mile, arriving at the western edge of plateau and open, scenic, rocky area—the result of early devastating forest fires. Trail follows open ridge for .25 mile in northerly direction, then turns right and north-east into hardwood forest. Trail follows a logging road for .5 mile, where it turns left sharply on an old logging-railroad grade which crosses aspen swamp.

Drinking water available along logging road.

Trail follows old grade for .25 mile, then turns right on old woods road for .25 mile. Trail intersects old logging-railroad grade and turns right on it in a southerly direction for .75 mile, then intersecting Route 44 and Refuge Trail. Trail now crosses Route 44, enters a mixed pine and oak forest, and travels in a southerly direction for 1 mile, intersecting Manor Fork Forestry Road and Hanowed Trail. Trail turns sharply right and moderately downgrade on old log trail for .25 mile to parking area and end of trail. Seven miles complete.

The Black Forest Ski Touring Trail is a 7-mile loop trail marked with blue blazes, crossing moderately rolling and flat terrain. The area is heavily forested and has several scenic vistas en route. Many interesting side trips can be taken for exploration by map and compass and also on other nearby marked state forest trails. Snowshoers are also welcome.

Elk Mountain Ski Center, Inc.–Uniondale

Suitable for novices and intermediate skiers. Length about 6 miles. This trail starts at the base lodge, traversing the lower T-bar area, climbs upward through forests to open meadows above parking lots. From there it follows the road coming into the area, staying about 50 yards above it. Approximately 2 miles from the starting point, it crosses the road and traverses hills and meadows on the opposite side of the mountain to descend into a small valley, then by serpentine trails brings you to the meadows below the area. After crossing a field you reach the starting point.

Delaware Water Gap

Approximately 6 miles following the Appalachian Trail above the Delaware Water Gap in New Jersey's Kittatinny Mountains. For both novices and intermediates.

Pocono Mountains

A favorite trip starting near the summit of Camelback, along the ridge and down through gently winding trails to Deep Lake with a long downhill run for a total of about 5 miles. For novices and intermediates.

Mount Pocono Region

Tour along the ridge at Devil's Hole, Mount Pocono Region, approximately 20 miles north of Stroudsburg. For novices and intermediates. Details: Jeff Wilhoyte, 36 Wyncroft Drive, Media, Pa. 19063. Information: Tel. 215-LO 6-8348.

VERMONT

Andover

Swedish Ski Club Lodge

More than 200 miles of ski-touring trails, all starting from and returning to the lodge. Two short trails, each 1.5 miles, both

215

wooded trails, very easy and suitable for beginners. Also, 3-, 6-, and 9-mile sanctioned trails. Andover is located between Chester and Weston, 8 miles north of Magic Mountain, 15 miles from Bromley, and 19 miles from Stratton. Nearest accommodations can be found at Corliss Motel, Meadow Motel, Chester Motor Inn, all in Chester, and the Weston Inn in Weston, Vt. 05143.

BENNINGTON

Dunville Hollow and Burgess Road Trail

Suitable for intermediate skiers. Distance about 7 miles. Starting point: Drive east from Bennington on Route 9 toward Prospect Mountain Ski Area. In about 5 miles, just before reaching a rock cut where the newer section of Route 9 begins to climb the mountain, you will see on the right a section of old highway, which leads a short distance to the Dunville Hollow Road. Cars may be parked on Route 9 at the old highway junction.

Finishing point: One mile east of Bennington on Route 9, at Williams IGA Store, bear right on Burgess Road. Drive toward the end of this road, parking near a white house on the left just before reaching the end of the plowed section of this road.

Begin tour at Dunville Hollow. Follow a section of old highway a short distance, cross bridge, then at a house bear right and proceed up the Dunville Hollow Road, which leads south up the valley of Stamford Stream. In about 3 miles from Route 9, just after passing the second of two hunting camps, bear right from the road onto a logging road, which immediately crosses Stamford Stream. Continue beside the stream on this logging road until a right bend is reached. Here join the blue-blazed Green Mountain Club Dunville Hollow Trail.

Following blue blazes, proceed uphill to the west along an old road. This was the Bennington–Heartwellville Stage Road of many years ago. The ascent on this road is steady but not steep.

Pass through a level, swampy area; then continue ascent. Upon reaching an open clearing, where there are good views of Glastenbury Mountain and other distant points, bear left, then right, soon crossing a small stream and area of frequent beaver activity.

After a final ascent, continue west on a wide logging road for about .25 mile.

The road now begins a long descent toward Bennington. A road junction is soon reached (to the left, this road leads south for 1.75 miles to Sucker Pond—another good route for ski touring).

Continue downhill on this road, which is drivable in the summer and thus is an excellent downhill ski run. About 1.75 miles from the bridge, reach the end of Burgess Road.

Bennington Area

Drive to end of Burgess Road and ski up Burgess Road, to above-mentioned road junction, take right fork, then tour south to Sucker Pond. Return same route. Total about 6.5 miles. There are 1.75 miles climbing, 3 miles level, 1.75 miles downhill.

BURKE MOUNTAIN

In the towns of Burke and Victory. About 6 miles of trails on state land in conjunction with 10 to 15 miles on Burke Mountain Recreation, Inc., land, Darling State Park and Victory State Forest.

Burke Mountain Area–East Burke

Burke Mountain offers wide terrain for ski touring. Its gently rolling hills spotted with large open meadows make it an exciting and stimulating place to enjoy this wonderful sport.

There are several trails at Burke, designed to provide some-

217

thing for each level of skier. Among these are the McGill Novice Trail, which has a rest cabin at its 3-mile point. Skiers may stay overnight at this cabin on a first-come, first-serve basis. Also included are the Four Hills Intermediate Trail and the Victory Expert Trail, which circles the mountain.

Instruction is available through the ski school, and it is available for groups, as well as private individuals.

The base lodge office will assist in making reservations for lodging accommodations. Has cabin for overnight stop 4 miles from base house. You may call 802-626-3305 or write to Burke Mountain Recreation, Inc., East Burke, Vt. 05832.

Brandon, Blueberry Hill Trail, Blueberry Hill Farm, near Goshen

A ski-touring center for the whole family, in the Green Mountains. Trails cover 25 miles. Besides the trails, much territory can be enjoyed by the ski tourer. All trails start at and return to Blueberry Hill. For the winter campers there is the Sucker Brook Shelter on the Long Trail. A two-day tour with an overnight stay at the Churchill Farm is possible. Equipment is for sale or rent at the Cross-country Ski Shop. Maps upon request. For more information and inn reservation call or write: Tony and Martha Clark, Blueberry Hill. PO Brandon, Vt. 05733. Tel. 802-247-6735.

Brattleboro

Ames Hill to South Pond and return. A novice trail 9 miles one way on unplowed roads. Start located 1.4 miles east of Marlboro and 4.9 miles west of West Brattleboro village on the Ames Hill Road. Follow state fishing access signs. Start between stone pillars on road branching off Ames Hill Road. A useful map is Brattleboro Quadrangle Vermont–New Hampshire 15 minute series topographic map, 1954 series AMS 6469 1 series V713.

Burrington Hill, near Whitingham

Suitable for novice skiers. Distance 2.5 miles. Trail begins at top of lift, goes down over a mowing to other side of mountain, up an old town road, around another mowing, and back to one of the trails, ending at base lodge.

Brookfield. Exits 4 and 5 Interstate 89.
Green Trails Rural Resort at the Floating Bridge.

Green Trails, located in the geographical center of Vermont, offers accommodations and meals in a country inn with complete ski-touring facilities, including miles of open land and marked trails, equipment sales and rentals, instruction, and workshops. Other recreational activities include snowshoeing, sleigh rides, tobogganing, and moonlight ski tours.

Green trails is also home base for the Central Vermont Winter Sports Club, organized in 1971 to promote ski touring and other winter sports in this area. Tel. 802-276-2012.

Can Am

This touring center, located next to the Jay Barn Inn, offers a Nordic specialty shop, ski-touring trails, instruction, and guided tours. William Perry, Manager, Can Am Ski Touring Center, Route 242, Jay, Vt. 05859. Tel. 802-988-4747.

Chittenden

The ski-touring area at Mountain Top Inn has several marked trails up to 6 miles in length. The Mountain Top Ski Touring Club accepts members. The inn offers accommodations and meals. It is located 8 miles east of Rutland. Instruction and rental of equipment are available. For information write or call Mountain Top Inn, Chittenden, Vt. 05737. Tel. 802-483-2311.

DANBY AREA

Two trails—suitable for intermediate skiers. When snow is deep, United States Forestry Service road to east from Mount Taber village is unplowed. From beginning to unplowed road, ascend about 2.5 miles (very scenic) to Long Trail. Continue on road for another mile to point where old Long Trail route turns south, on woods road. Descend to Big Branch Bridge; then go downstream to shelter. Total about 8 miles. Uphill on roads 2.5 miles, level-road walking 2 miles, down old road .5 mile, descend unplowed road 2.5 miles.

DANBY–WALLINGFORD AREA

Ascend unplowed United States Forestry Service road mentioned above to Long Trail. Go north on Long Trail to Little Rock Pond (two shelters). Descend Homer Stone Brook Trail to South Wallingford. Total about 7.5 miles. Uphill on unplowed road 2.5 miles, near-level Long Trail 2.5 miles, descend trail 2.5 miles.

Jay area is the starting point of a large number of ski-touring trails consisting of logging trails, unplowed dirt roads, hiking trails, all marked by the North Country Ski Touring Club. All trails are for novices and intermediates. All trails start at Route 242 (the road leads west from 101 to Jay Peak).

Starting points as follows:

Chalet Edelweiss, one of the trails leading to a sugar shack.

Jay Barn Village.

Sonnenhof Inn, one of the trails for intermediates including bushwhacking.

Snow Cap Lodge, two trails leading to sugar shacks. Schneehuette, 2 miles west from Jay, trail leading to Vermont's largest elm tree.

All places have rental equipment.

EAST BURKE–DARION INN–SKI-TOURING CENTER

The inn's trail system snakes through the 15,000 acres which made up the Elmer Darling Farm. Daily instruction is offered in group or private lessons. Ski-week programs are available. Lodging can be provided in either private rooms or in the ski dorm. Winter camping is permitted for the more rugged individuals. The cross-country shop has sales and rentals of ski-touring equipment. No trail fees. Call for reservations: 802-626-5641.

FAYSTON–TUCKER HILL LODGE CROSS-COUNTRY CENTER

Experienced guides and instructors are available for touring and racing. Rental and sales of ski-touring equipment in the sales and rental shop. Meals and lodging available. For information contact Tom and Jane Martin, Tucker Hill Lodge, Route 17, Fayston (PO Waitsfield), Vt. 05673. Tel. 802-496-3983.

KILLINGTON SKI AREA, KILLINGTON

Ski-touring facilities at Killington Ski Area, Killington, five miles of ski-touring trails for beginners and intermediate skiers. Trails marked with signs. Additional trails are being planned. Skis (also "no-wax" skis) are for sale or for rent in the ski shop in the Snowshed Lodge for adults and children; also bindings, boots, poles, and wax.

Instructors available for group or private lessons. All-day tours. Map of touring trails can be picked up at welcome center in Snowshed Lodge.

For information: Miss Janice Fleetwood, Killington Ski Area, Killington, Vt. 05751. Tel. 802-422-3333.

LONDONDERRY

Viking Ski Touring Center. Little Pond Road

Six trails varying in length from .1 mile to 8 miles. Race course with set tracks available for practice and working out. Touring trails vary in difficulty, but most are suitable for novices.

The 8-mile touring trail starts at shop, circles around Cobble Hill through rolling, wooded terrain. About a 2-mile run through fields before reentering the woods and returning to the Viking Ski Shop.

A heated waxing hut, equipment rentals, instruction, a fully equipped shop, guided tours from one-half day to three days long are available at the center. Winter camping equipment available for rent, including such items as tents, sleeping bags, and backpacks. Tel. 802-824-3933.

LOWELL

Road 58, starting point about 1 mile west of the village, where road is unplowed during winter. Length about 6 miles to a point about 2 miles east of Montgomery Center, from which point road will be plowed. Eastern part between point near Lowell and summit of about 3 miles, which is Hazen's Notch Road, is quite level and ideal for novices. Beyond, the North Road descends rather steeply, 20 to 30 percent, with sharp turns. This part good for intermediate. Advisable to go from east to west, otherwise one will have a long, steep climb from the point near Montgomery Center to summit. The road most probably is also used by snowmobilers, but is wide enough to make it reasonably good for ski tourers. Lowell is located on Route 100, about 20 miles north of Morrisville and about 30 miles north of Stowe.

LUDLOW-OKEMO—THE FAMILY MOUNTAIN

Fire tower to Base Lodge via 4.5-mile packed road. A lazy intermediate's dream. A short uphill trek from top of upper chair to a 36-degree view which includes the White and Adirondack mountains. Then an easy 4.5 downhill miles to starting point.

Base Lodge via Work Road to West Villa go and return. Intermediate. Easy uphill (or via poma lifts) via Mountain

Road (1.5 miles) to Work Road (flat 1.5 miles), to Sachem (down .3 mile) to new unplowed residential road (flat .75 mile) and return via roads and fields (downhill 1 mile).

Base Lodge to flood-control dam and return. Beginners. Skirt parking lot to footbridge. Go through woods, large open field and across secondary road to lake and open area. From here one may either return or, after short climb, discover another, far larger rolling field area (1 mile in length), off which are various woods roads.

The Okemo area includes a variety of terrains, including downhill and through-the-woods exploring.

Instruction is available, as well as a variety of guided tours. Day trips, with appropriate menu, can be arranged.

The ski shop carries a full complement of lightweight touring equipment for rental or purchase.

For further information, lodging help, etc., call 802-228-5321 or write Okemo RFD 1, Ludlow, Vt. 05149.

MAD RIVER GLEN AREA–WAITSFIELD

Suitable for good intermediate and expert skiers only. Trail starts at top of Mad River double chair lift, at 3,060-foot altitude. It is well marked with red rectangles and long white or blue cloth markers. It is recommended that no less than three in a party attempt this trail. From chair lift go north on a Long Trail about .5 mile, over undulating terrain along the ridge of the Green Mountains. At the touring trail sign pointing left take the bypass downhill, and continue until the Long Trail is again joined; turn right, going uphill about 100 yards, and turn left, as directed, descending again. Eventually, the trail nears the Mc-Cullough Turnpike, just below Appalachian Gap. After passing through a shallow valley, the trail joins the Snail, which leads back to the base (1,600 feet). Note: Following the Long Trail through to Appalachian Gap is not recommended, as the foot trail passes over Stark's Wall, which is *not* skiable under any conditions. Deep snow conditions are needed because some of the terrain is rough. Notify Mad River Glen Area management before attempting trip.

There is also good touring to be found on unplowed roads across fields and pastures on Bragg Hill, north of the access road to the area (Mill Brook Road), and east of Waitsfield Common. About .75 mile down the road from the Mad River base area, a woods road leads off to the north. This slopes upward about a mile, into wooded valley laced with logging roads.

Madonna–Vasa Trail–
Cambridge, Underhill, Stowe

Twenty miles of moderate-to-difficult trails, including the 12-mile Madonna–Vasa Race Course between Madonna parking lot and the mountain road in Underhill. Expert skiers may continue from Underhill, climb the Notch south of Mansfield, and end at the tollhouse in Stowe or continue with trails of the Trapp Family Lodge. Marking is incomplete, and those trails should be used only if accompanied by persons familiar with them.

Manchester–The Equinox House

Over 12 miles trail network is planned with kilometer workers at intervals on the long loops, also a sled-prepared track on at least 6 miles of this network to be maintained. For information: The Equinox House, Manchester, Vt. 05254. Tel. 802-362-1640.

Manchester Depot

Trail starts on Routes 11 and 30, about a mile east of Manchester, where the road crosses the Battenkill River (also railroad tracks). The trail makes a loop with a place to get on and off about midway. The loop can be completed on foot in about two hours and finishes about 200 to 300 yards from the starting point. Good for novices and up (not for beginners). Essentially it first goes up one side of the Battenkill River, crosses it, and comes back. Part of it is through some rolling meadows. Instruction, sale and rental of equipment. Details: Battenkill Sports, routes 11 and 30, Manchester Depot, Vt. 05255. Phone Robin Verner, 802-362-2734.

MANCHESTER–PERU

Three Trails Suitable for Intermediate Skiers

Manchester Area. Drive to Manchester Depot, then east to Chalet Motel, turning on dirt road to its end at foot of mountain. Park near white house. Ascend logging road (which is unplowed) for 1.75 miles. Reach Long Trail and Prospect Rock, a fine lookout! Swezey Camp .9 mile farther can be used for cooking dinner. Total about 5.5 miles. Climbing for 1.75 miles, 2 miles level, 1.75 miles downhill.

Bromley Area. Ride up Bromley Mountain chair lift. Ski down Long Trail to Bromley Camp and Route 11, west of Bromley Ski Area. Utilize ski trail for a distance, balance via trail through woods, distance about 3 miles, all downhill. Follow White Long Trail blazes.

Hapgood Pond Area. (near Peru): From highway, drive north on dirt road to road junction; then walk west on unplowed United States Forestry Service road to Mad Tom Notch; use shelter nearby for lunch. Total about 4 miles—uphill to shelter, downhill on return trip. For the adventurous, the trip can continue west down the old Dorset–Peru road; from the top of the Notch to East Dorset is about 4.5 miles. The latter must be done when the snow is deep and the stream is frozen.

MARLBORO–BRATTLEBORO

Ames Hill to South Pond and Return

This is a level, gentle, wide automobile road maintained in summer. It is unplowed in the winter, but sometimes snowmobiles use this access road to the state fishing facility of South Pond. It is an in-and-out track-out trail, wooded on both sides and wind-protected. Relatively high elevation—1,674 feet—makes skiable snow available early and late in winter. Length is .9 mile one way. Definitely novice. Starting point is located 1.4 miles east of Marlboro and 4.9 miles west of West Brattleboro village on the Ames Hill Road. Follow state fishing access signs, start between stone pillars on road branching off Ames Hill Road. See Brattleboro Quadrangle Vermont–New Hampshire 15 minute series topographic map, 1954 Series AMS 6469 1 series V713.

Morgan Center. On Route 111

A few miles northeast of this village is located Wildwood Valley, with an excellent network of touring trails partly marked.

Mountain Meadows

Secluded in the heart of Killington Basin, this ski-touring center, established by two former Olympians, offers a combination of activities. Trails through the Vermont woods are unlimited, and the shop offers information, equipment, and accessories. Accommodations at the Mountain Meadows Lodge. William Dunnington, Manager, Mountain Meadows Ski Touring Center, c/o Mountain Meadows Lodge, Killington, Vt. 05751. Tel. 802-775-2843.

MOUNT SNOW AREA

Base Lodge—Trail of 2.5 kilometers at Mount Snow for touring and Nordic NASTAR events. Somerset Reservoir Trail.

Rudge Trail connecting Mount Snow and Haystack Mountain, Mount Snow Golf Course.

Green Mountain House

In West Wardsboro at junction of Route 100 and Stratton Road. Inn specializes in accommodations for ski tourers. Trails at Mount Snow just 5 miles to the south of the Long Trail or Stratton Mountain to the west. Logging-road trails, woodland trails, field crossings, and unplowed dirt roads are in the immediate vicinity of the inn. (Maps are available.) Most popular is a 4.5-mile Podunk Road and trail through nearby maple-sugar stands.

South Londonderry

Trails originating at Woody's Cracker Barrel, junction of routes 30 and 100, Rawsonville. Details and map of trails available by writing Woody's Cracker Barrel, South Londonderry, Vt. 05155.

1. Close-in system of trails including practice runs on meadows, approximately 8 miles total. Several miles kept tracked for technique or race training.

2. Continuing from head of close-in trail system along old West Hill Road, with crossing of Pinnacle Ridge and descent to Pikes Falls Valley possible. Tour can then continue to North Cemetery and thus to Stratton, 11 miles one way. Moderate technically, but considerable climbing either way.

3. Trip to Gale Meadows and return; gentle terrain, length 6 miles.

4. Continuation of above to either Peru or Landgrove; thus longer tours up to 15 miles (one way) possible.

5. Old West River railway roadbed. Gentle tours can originate from South Londonderry or Rawsonville. The roadbed extends down West River to Jamaica, past the Ball Mountain flood control dam. Fifteen miles one way. Tour can originate from Rawsonville and follow Winhall River to West River and then branch off to South Londonderry or south to Jamaica.

6. Branching off from old West River railway roadbed after the crossing of Pratt Bridge is an old logging road which can be followed back to South Londonderry, or alternately used to cross over the saddle between Globe and Shatterack mountains into Windham. Descent can then be made to Jamaica along old logging roads on Turkey Mountain.

STRATTON AREA

Drive to West Wardsboro, then west to Stratton village and end of plowed road at Stratton Mountain Scout Reservation. Ski unplowed road, then Long Trail, to Stratton Pond (one cabin and two shelters). Total 8 miles. Very gradual trail 7 miles, unplowed road 1 mile.

Stratton Mountain Ski-Touring Trails

All trails mentioned below start at the Stratton Corporation development in Bondville. Ski-touring equipment for rent at Stratton Mountain Ski Area.

Stratton–Summit Trail

Length 1.5 miles round trip, very little climbing. Suitable for novices or intermediate skiers. Summit Trail runs due south from upper terminal of chair lifts No. 3 and 5 to the south summit fire tower (elevation 3,936 foot). The tower provides a 360-degree view. Total time for round trip about 1½ hours.

Stratton–The Long Trail

Length 3 miles. Suitable for experts only. The Long Trail runs due south from the fire tower to the Kelley Stand Road. This is downhill all the way (2,000 feet). The trail is narrow and steep in places and should be attempted only by experts accompanied by a Stratton ski patrolman. A patrolman will be supplied if sufficient notice is given to the ski patrol. Automobile transportation must be arranged for return to the Stratton Ski Area.

Stratton–North Cemetery Trail

Length 1.5 miles. For novices, with additional 4.5 miles for intermediate skiers. This trail begins at the bottom of No. 4 T-bar (just above the Lift Line Lodge). Follow the red blazes to the cemetery. An easy, slightly downhill trail, excellent for novices. Novices can return to the ski area from this point. More advanced skiers can continue down the mountain road. Here the trail comes into the Mountain Road, an unplowed, unpaved road leading into the paved Pikes Falls Road, 1 mile below the cemetery. Stratton's work road comes into Pikes Falls Road .25 mile to the north of the junction of the Mountain Road and Pikes Falls Road.

A 5- to 6-mile tour can be made beginning and ending at the T-bar with only a 200-foot descent and ascent.

Stratton–Kidder Brook Jeep Trail

Length 2 miles. Suitable for intermediates. This trail leads uphill from the North Cemetery paralleling Kidder Brook, in a northwesterly direction. Connects with Logging Road for 1,000-foot steep climb swinging north and northeast downhill back to the North Cemetery Trail. Detailed map available from Ski Touring Council, R. F. Mattesich, West Hill Road, Troy, Vt. 05868.

SAW MILL

For a profound change of pace, in an area noted solely for downhill skiing, you can visit the little touring center at the Saw Mill Farm Inn. Completely equipped, including equipment, rentals, instruction, and guided tours. Accommodations are available in the inn. Scott Leake, Saw Mill Ski Touring Center, The Inn at Saw Mill, West Dover, Vt. 05356. Tel. 802-464-2782.

SERENDIPITY

Located in the heart of Manchester Center, this ski-touring center offers a complete facility for touring, touring equipment and accessories. A complete line of ski rentals. Instruction and guided tours are also available. You may tour right into the village and its environs. Also, guided tours are possible both on the Long Trail and in the Merck Forest. Nancy Worsoe, Manager, Serendipity Ski Touring Center, Eleven Thirty Corner, Manchester, Vt. 05255. Tel. 802-362-3272.

STOWE

Located in Stowe Center, on the Mountain Road (Route 108) in Stowe, this ski-touring center offers a list of winter activities. Equipment and accessories are available for purchase or rental. Guided tours, instruction by certified instructors, a heated pool and sauna, a convenient children's care center, restaurant/lounge, and delicatessen. Kim Rode, Manager, Stowe Ski Touring Center, Stowe Center, Box 1308, Stowe, Vt. 05672. Tel. 802-253-4592 or 4631.

Stowe–Touring Trail from Trapp Family Lodge in Stowe to Bolton Ski Area

The trail consists of three sections: (1) from the Trapp Lodge in Stowe to the top of Bolton Mountain; (2) from Bolton Mountain to Bryant Lodge; (3) from Bryant Lodge to Little River. The trail is marked for hiking. There are blue painted blazes at eye level for ski touring, and red plastic rectangles at 8 feet. The trail system is almost 18 miles long and offers views of Lake Champlain, Mount Mansfield, Camel's Hump, Little River Reservoir, Ricker and Cotton Brook basins, and the Worcester Range. For a long, yet gentle run, ride the lift at Bolton Valley to the top of Ricker Mountain, and ski gradually downhill either toward the Trapp Lodge or Little River. For the novice, a short but scenic run is from the top of Ricker Mountain to Bryant Lodge and back to the base of the lifts. For the expert, the trail could be run from either end toward the middle. The climb is not steep, but very long. A word of caution, however: These trails are a long way from civilization, and unless you are an expert skier or with someone who knows the trail, do not attempt it, as weather can get very bad in the high mountain areas. For further information contact either the Trapp Lodge in Stowe or the Bolton Valley Ski Area. Maps are available through the Forest and Parks Department on a limited basis. Contact William Moulton, State Land Forester, Agency of Environmental Conservation, Montpelier, Vt. 05602.

Stowe Area–Mount Mansfield Summit Trip

Suitable for novices; recommended for advanced skiers. Distance 2 miles or more if desired. Take chair lift to the Octagon hut; follow the Toll Road (going north about .75 mile) up to the old hotel site (now a TV transmitting station), and continue to the west side, leaving the forest and reaching the ledges, for fine view across western Vermont, Lake Champlain, and the Adirondacks. Ski to the east side of the mountain, past the radar station for a splendid view of Mount Washington and the Presidential Range in New Hampshire. A good spot for lunch. Touring time about 1 ½ hours.

SPRUCE PEAK TO SMUGGLER'S NOTCH POMA LIFT AND RETURN

Suitable for novices, intermediate, and advanced skiers. Distance about 2 miles. Proceed from top of Spruce Peak chair lift on trail to Smugglers' Notch upper poma lift. The section around Sterling Pond is extremely scenic, and the entire trip can easily be negotiated by the average intermediate or careful beginner. Returning from Smugglers' Notch, you can connect with the Sterling Trail down Spruce Peak. Advanced skiers may extend the trip by running down the Smugglers' Notch trails to the Jeffersonville (Ski-Ways Inc.) Lodge, return on their poma lifts, and then run down to the bottom of Spruce Peak. This round trip requires about 2 hours, depending on length of lift lines.

MOUNT MANSFIELD

Rim Rock Trail to Taft Lodge and Perry Merrill back to parking area. This is a trip for the upper-intermediate to expert skier. It is all through spruce forest along a 1,000-foot-high ledge. You have to get down the Nose to Station 11 (the upper part of the slalom glades). Here look for the trail junction of Perry Merrill and Rim Rock (well brushed and marked with blazes and red plastic strips).

Take Rim Rock, and at a gradual grade after 1.5 miles, you will get to Taft Lodge. It is possible to continue on to explore the Eagle Pass to the west with its Lakes of the Clouds trail.

Return to Taft Lodge, and take the Perry Merrill back to the parking lot (about 2 miles) with a drop of 1,800 feet. This trip should be taken, preferably, in the company of someone who has been over the trail.

A good variation (for experts only) is a trip up to the hotel site. Then ski-walk 1.2 miles to the Chin (4,393 feet). Several hundred feet south of the peak is a very steep gully (Profanity Trail) which will take you down the east side of the pass and to Taft Lodge.

RUPERT

Merck Forest Foundation

A 2,600-acre private park dedicated to the preservation of natural values and traditional forest recreations. All motorized vehicles prohibited. Hikers, ski tourers, and snowshoers are welcome.

Contains 26 miles of forest roads suitable for all levels of skiing ability. Wide, open meadows and excellent views from several lookout points.

Located about 10 miles northwest from Manchester Center, Vt. Vermont Route 30, and 15 miles northwest from Salem, N.Y., New York Route 22. Entrance is at the height of land on an unnumbered route joining West Rupert, East Rupert, and Dorset, Vt.

STOWE AREA

Stowe–The Farm Motor Inn & Country Club

Located 6 minutes north of Stowe on Route 100. Tel. 802-

888-3525. Gentle rolling hills of golf courses and logging roads of wooded farmland make up the miles of cross-country trails. The restaurant and motel complex are the starting and finishing points. Trails offer woods for protection on windy days and the gentle, open slopes of the golf course for the warm sunny days. Rental and sales for all cross-country equipment along with box lunches are available. Trail maps upon request.

Stowe–Trapp Family Lodge

The first cross-country ski-touring center in the East offers 40 miles of trails well marked with signs and markers. New trail to Bolton Valley Ski Area. (Experts only unless guided.) Many open fields for novices. Rental and sale of touring equipment. Instruction and guided tours. Cabin serving lunch located 4 miles in the woods. Program Director Larry Damon. Trapp Family Lodge, Stowe, Vt. 05672. Tel. 802-253-4806.

WARREN

Sugarbush Inn maintains excellent trail system. Instruction, sales, and rentals.

WATERBURY CENTER–SKI HOSTEL LODGE

Lodge surrounded by acres of beautiful ski-touring terrain affording beautiful views. Fine trails (not marked). Accommodations and meals available. Ten minutes from Stowe on Route 100. For details: Martha Guthridge. Tel. 802-244-8859.

WEST WARDSBORO

See Mount Snow Area and Stratton Area (pages 226–229).

WILMINGTON–THE MOUNTAIN ROAD SHOP

A complete cross-country ski shop owned and operated by Jim and Tricia Meyer. Located .75 mile north of Wilmington on Route 100. Sales of touring, light touring, and racing skis. Instructors give group or private lessons from shop. Also take groups (maximum of six) overnight camping; all equipment is supplied. Catalogue and information sheets are available on request. Contact The Mountain Road Shop, Route 100, Wilmington, Vt. 05363. Tel. 802-464-8646.

WOODFORD, VERMONT AT VERMONT SKI CAMP, PROSPECT MOUNTAIN

Vermont Ski Camp–Greenwood Lodge offers individuals and groups use of a variety of wooded and open trails with varied terrain on 120 acres adjacent to Prospect Ski Mountain. Maps available at lodge or ski area. The ski camp caters primarily to youth groups and offers varied skiing and recreational activities. Dorm type of facilities. Box 246, Bennington, Vt. 05201.

WOODSTOCK–BARNARD AREA. THE SKY LINE TRAIL

Trails are suitable for intermediate skiers.

Woodstock to Barnard. Orange on top of sign. Barnard to Woodstock, blue on top of sign. Best run north to south—for less climb, more downhill.

Amity Pond to Webster Hill. Approximately 2 miles. Trail starts at fence opening on west side of Sky Line Road. Sign reads FOOT AND HORSEBACK TRAIL. Turn northwest through open pasture to stone fence. After passing through fence opening, turn south, passing Amity Pond. Continue south downgrade to a clump of birches. Turn southeast and cross two stone fences enclosing a lane. Cross a small swamp, climbing slightly, and head south through open fields with some hardwoods. Shortly after passing a fence opening there is an abrupt turn west, followed immediately by a return to the southerly direction over rolling terrain and open pastures with fences and white-pine thickets on the west. Cross a lane and several fences, and go east toward Allen log house (above and east of trail), arriving at a short lane near Haydock House. Here the trail joins the Sky Line

234

Road, not plowed beyond this point. Trail follows the road, generally south, to intersecting Webster Hill Road.

Webster Hill to Home of Thomas Harvey. Approximately .9 Miles. A protected road through hardwoods, slightly rolling and for the most part below a ridge to the west. The last few hundred feet are plowed from the Barclay Jones house driveway to the Harvey Farm.

WOODSTOCK

Harvey Farm to Gregg House. Approximately 1 Mile

Turn east between Harvey farm buildings, equipment shed on left. Trail sign is on large maple tree near shed. Short uphill section skirts brush area and wire fence to the south. Pass through wooden gate at top of rise, then follow lane easterly to intersection marked by wooden gate and signs, then turn south and continue on wooded lane to Gregg House.

Gregg House to Churchill House. Approximately 2.75 Miles

Trail follows old wooden road southwest, then south. The latter portion descending on steady slight grade. From Gregg House, road rises for short distance and is sometimes plowed; trail follows open field beside road.

Churchill House to Suicide Six. Approximately .25 Miles

Approaching Churchill House, turn right (west) at sign, and cross brook at bridge. Follow trail signs, traversing around side of hill above sugar house, then down through pastures toward Suicide Six acres.

Woodstock Inn.

The golf course on the inn offers ski touring; 3 miles of trails especially for novices. The Golf Club has rental equipment and offers ski-touring instruction and guided tours during the season. Call George Williamson, Manager. 802-457-2112.

SKI-TOURING TRAILS MAINTAINED BY VERMONT DEPARTMENT OF FORESTS AND PARKS

Mount Mansfield State Forest

In the town of Underhill. Five miles of trails linking Madonna-Vasa Trail, through Underhill State Park, with Trapp Family Lodge Trail at Nebraska Notch. An additional trail will connect the Bolton Valley Ski Area with the Trapp Trail to Nebraska Notch. This trail traverses rugged terrain and is recommended only for experienced tourers.

Granville Gulf State Park

Puddledock Trail, 2.8 miles, just east of Route 100 in Granville Gulf. The beginning point to the Puddledock Ski Trail is on Route 100, approximately 7 miles south of the village of Warren. The parking area and identifying sign are on the east side of the highway. A brochure distribution box is located a short distance up the trail.

Okemo State Forest

In the town of Ludlow and Mount Holly. Trails are planned in cooperation with Okemo Mountain, Inc.

Woodford State Park

In Woodford. Connecting with old roads used by skiers in Stamford, Pownal, and Bennington.

Camel's Hump State Park

In Bolton, Duxbury, Huntington, Fayston. Potential for 50 to 60 miles of trails without interference by snowmobiles.

WEST VIRGINIA

BERKELEY SPRINGS. COLD RUN VALLEY ROAD, THE COOLFONT RE'CREATION, INC.

Maintains net of ski-touring trails, also offers skijoering.

MONONGAHELA NATIONAL FOREST

Has miles of unplowed roads well suited for ski touring. Spruce Knob, the highest point in West Virginia (4,863 feet), can be reached on touring skis, as can the Dolly Sods and Shavers Fork country area. Both offer trails for ski touring. Maps available from National Forest Service, Washington, D.C.

THE MIDWEST AND OTHER AREAS
MINNESOTA

THEODORE WIRTH PARK (PUBLIC)

Public golf course owned by Minneapolis Park Board.
Terrain—Most open, some woods, varying hills.
Trail—One trail, intermediate, 2 miles long. Begins in front of chalet, goes past outrun of ski jump and up road to left.
Location—On Glenwood Parkway between U.S. 55 and Golden Valley Road, 2 miles west of downtown.
Comments—Refreshments available at park chalet. Some unofficial "trails" of easy level may be found south of chalet.

JONATHAN (OAKVIK HOUSE) (PUBLIC)

Ski area managed by North Star Ski Touring Club.
Terrain—Scenic and varied hill, fields, woods.
Trails—Main trail several miles long, fairly easy, begins behind house and goes north across railroad tracks. Short competition trail around lake west of house.
Location—Southwest of Minneapolis. Take Minnesota 5 west

The lazy way to go ski touring—behind a snowmobile—combines one of the oldest winter sports with one of the newest.

Courtesy Norwegian National Tourist Office

from 494. Turn south on 41, go 1.8 miles to Oakvik House on west side of road (big sign).

Accommodations—Oakvik House is open to all skiers during most club events; to members only at other times. It can also be used by nonmember groups with special permission.

Comments—Kitchen facilities available to members. Great place for quick, fun cross-country outings. Please carry garbage home.

Parking—Do not park on Highway 41 because of police surveillance.

Twin Cities Public Golf Course (Public)

All Minneapolis and St. Paul public golf courses are open to cross-country skiers. Please stay off all greens, even those which are covered with brush. No camping, fires, or any type of sled allowed.

Terrain—Ideal conditions, ranging from easy to advanced, with snowmobiles banned.

Minneapolis Golf Courses

Columbia—3300 Central NE.
Gross—St. Anthony and 22d Avenue NE.
Hiawatha—4553 Longfellow Avenue.
Meadowbrook—201 Meadowbrook (St. Louis Park).
Wirth—Glenwood Parkway and Plymouth Avenue N.

St. Paul Golf Course

Como—Larpenteur Ave. and Como Avenue.
Highland—Snelling Ave. and Montreal Avenue.
Phelan—Larpenteur Ave. and Highway 61.

Washington County Parkland (Public)

Park development area near metropolitan area.
Terrain—Varied open and wooded, hilly.

Trails—No established trails, but 4 or 5 miles of skiing possible. Intermediate.

Location—Distance 10 miles from St. Paul. Take U.S. 61 to Cottage Grove, left onto County 19 at Chemolite Plant. East 1.5 miles to turnaround; parking area to right.

Itasca State Park

Terrain—Intermediate to expert, in the south part of the park. However, easy trails can be found around the Wilderness Bay Resort, a good place to stay.

Trails—Well-marked trails numbered for varying distances. Through beautiful virgin pine and small lakes. Get map from State of Minnesota, Itasca State Park.

Location—U.S. Highway 10 to Little Falls, Motley, Staples, and Wadena. Turn right in Wadena on Highway 71 to Park Rapids. Continue north on 71 approximately 20 miles to park. About 210 miles from the Twin Cities.

Accommodations—Wilderness Bay Resort recommended. Reasonable cabins and meals at the lodge. About 4 miles from the south boundary of the park. Tel. 218-732-4865.

Comments—Snowmobiles prohibited on park trails, but they will be on the lakes.

Grand Marais, Minnesota

Terrain—Everything from beginners to expert, depending on the trail chosen. Many old logging roads, wide enough for safety. Most of the trails are up high from Lake Superior back on the ridges.

Trails—From 3 or 4 miles to Routes 17 and 20. Well marked on a map of Cook County available from the Ski Club in Grand Marais and indications how to get to them. There are at least twenty trails in use now, starting from the Sawbill Trail up to the Grand Portage Trail.

Location—North shore of Lake Superior about 260 miles from the Twin Cities. Freeway to Two Harbors.

Accommodations—Many motels, cabins, and hotels found in Grand Marais and restaurants open in winter.

Comments—Some of the best ski touring in this area. A very cooperative ski club in Grand Marais to help visitors enjoy the skiing. Call John Viren at the Trading Post, or Norris Hystad, attorney in Grand Marais, for information.

HENNEPIN COUNTY PARK SYSTEM (PUBLIC)

This is a system of park units, 1,000 to 3,000 acres in size, located near the north, west, and south borders of Hennepin County. Five of the parks have 8 to 10 miles of trails designed especially for ski touring.

Terrain—Mostly gently rolling, with scattered patches of woods, lakes, and fields. Eighty percent or more of each park is kept undeveloped except for trails.

Trails—Easy to intermediate. The skier has a choice of loops: 1½ to 2 miles, 3 to 5 miles, and 5 to 7 miles. All trails are well marked.

Location—(Park units with ski-touring trails distance given from center of Minneapolis.)

Hyland Lake: South of I 494 off Normandale Road, 12 miles.

Carver: West on Minnesota 5, 20 miles.

Morris T. Baker: West on U.S. 12 or Minnesota 55 and County 24, 18 miles.

Lake Rebecca: West on Minnesota 55, 25 miles.

Elm Creek: North on Minnesota 152, 15 miles.

Comments—These parks are some of the very few in Minnesota with trails set up especially for skiers. Nature centers at Hyland and Carver parks. A $1 per day car fee at each park. A $5 seasonal permit is good at all parks. Inquire about equipment rental at Hyland, Carver, and Morris T. Baker. Call 473-4693 for more information.

ALPENHORN (PUBLIC)

Privately operated area for downhill and cross-country skiing open to the public.

Terrain—Varied; hilly, open, wooded.

Trails—No trails yet established, but three areas provide unlimited opportunities for everything from easy to advanced skiing.

Accommodations—Meals, lodging available in Paynesville.

Location—Near Lake Koronis, Paynesville, Minnesota, on U.S. 55, about 100 miles west of Twin Cities.

Comments—This is a new area and has not yet been fully explored for ski touring.

> For information contact:
> Marcel Kobberdahl
> 612-933-1995 (Eden Prairie)
> or write: PO Box 105
> Paynesville, Minn. 56362
> Phone: 612-243-4670 or 243-4579

SHERBURNE NATIONAL WILDLIFE REFUGE (PUBLIC)

Terrain—Mostly wooded, generally level.

Trails—Three connecting loop trails, easy, giving distances of 1, 1.75, and 2.5 miles.

Location—Distance 55 miles north of Twin Cities. Take U.S. 169, 14 miles north of Elk River, go left on County 9, 5 miles to refuge headquarters.

Accommodations—None. Bring a lunch and picnic in the snow.

BANNING STATE PARK (KETTLE RIVER) (PUBLIC)

Terrain—Wooded, level highland with a steep river gorge cutting through it.

Trails—Two or three trails of between 1 and 3 miles length, easy to intermediate.

Location—Distance 100 miles from Twin Cities. Take I-35 to Minnesota 23 near Sandstone, go east 1 mile.

Accommodations—Bring lunch.

Comments—Snowmobile traffic is light before noon. Check with park ranger about thin ice on the Kettle River.

ST. CROIX STATE PARK (PUBLIC)

Terrain—Rolling, wooded country, some river-bottom area.

Trails—Several ski trails ranging from easy to intermediate.

Location—Distance 90 miles from Twin Cities. Take I-35 to Hinckley, 48 east to park entrance.

Accommodations—Camping is possible. Bring lunch, as there are no convenient restaurants.

Comments—Could be fine area if the snowmobile traffic were controlled.

CLOQUET (PUBLIC)

Public ski trail owned by city of Cloquet

Terrain—Scenic, wooded, hilly.

Trails—Two trails, 1.5 and 3 miles long, fairly easy (watch for a few tough turns).

Location—Near Driftwood Motel on Highway 33 as you enter Cloquet. Ask directions at motel.

Accommodations—Driftwood Motel, Cloquet. Nice rooms, about $6 per person. Good steak house a block from the motel.

Comments—There is a $1 fee to use the trails. Check race schedule beforehand. (Area is closed during race meets.)

GOOSEBERRY STATE PARK (PUBLIC)

State park on north shore of Lake Superior.

Terrain—Wooded, gently rolling except for a few very steep sections.

Trails—Many narrow trails, ranging from easy to advanced. Caution: Some trails have steep drops or sharp turns which may be hazardous.

Location—On North Shore Highway 12 miles east of Two Harbors, Minn. (I-35 to U.S. 61).

Accommodations—Motels in Duluth and Two Harbors.

Comments—Most trails are located between U.S. 61 and the lake.

ELY HIDDEN VALLEY (PUBLIC)

Downhill and cross-country area close to Ely.

Terrain—Scenic and varied, lakes, hills, woods.

Trails—Variety of trails ranging from easy and intermediate touring to a moderate competition trail.

Location—Distance 250 miles from Twin Cities. Follow 169 east from Ely about a mile to Hidden Valley sign and turnoff to south.

Accommodations—Sleeping-bag space in chalet, meals furnished for groups up to 35 people. Chalet cannot be reserved exclusively and is used by downhillers during the day.

Comments—Nice area to wait out a blizzard.

ELY–BURNTSIDE NORTH (PUBLIC)

Camp owned by YMCA (YMCA Camp du Nord).

Terrain—Varied hills, lakes.

Trails—Many and varied, mostly easy, logging roads, portage trails, lakes (portage trails have some difficult parts).

Location—Distance 260 miles from Twin Cities. Take 169 east from Ely, turn left onto County 88, follow Echo Trail 9 miles to North Arm Road, go 3.5 miles to YMCA Camp du Nord.

Accommodations—Sleeping-bag space for 25 in log building with cooking facilities (no electricity or plumbing). Bring food.

Rent is $80 per weekend for entire log building with 20 people or less. Contact:

> Camp Du Nord Camp Director
> St. Paul YMCA
> St. Paul, Minn.
> Phone: 222-0771

Lodging and meals also available in Ely.

VAL CHATEL (PUBLIC)

Downhill and cross-country ski area.

Terrain—Gentle hills and flat, abandoned railroad grades.

Trails—Loop around lake north of chalet. Easy, with a few fair hills, long railroad grade. Area south of chalet has woods, snowmobile trails.

Location—Distance 200 miles from Twin Cities near Park Rapids. Take U.S. 10 west to Wadena, U.S. 71 north to Park Rapids. Turn east on 34, 6 blocks, then north on Lake George Road about 14 miles.

Accommodations—Traveler's Motel/Restaurant in Park Rapids. Good food also at Val Chatel, and lodging may be available this season. Contact owner:

> Rod Peterson
> Val Chatel
> Park Rapids, Minn. 56470

Comments—Good for groups up to 20 people.

PILLSBURY STATE PARK (PUBLIC, OPEN)

Terrain—Everything that 14,000 acres of north-central Minnesota can offer.

Trails—Many old logging roads for easy skiing. One trail 25 miles long for intermediate–advanced skiers.

Location—Distance 10 miles northwest of Brainerd on Highway 210. Groups must check in at the Pillager Ranger Station on 210. Trail maps available there.

Accommodations—Camp in the park, or stay in motels in Brainerd.

Comments—Like most of the state's larger and more attractive parks, Pillsbury is overrun by snowmobiles.

MARINE-ON-ST. CROIX (PRIVATE)

Private ski area owned by Ralph Malmberg (Malmberg's General Store), Marine-on-St. Croix, Minn. 55047.

Terrain—Secluded woods along St. Croix bottoms.

Trails—Two trails: 3 to 4 miles on Wisconsin side, 4 to 5 miles on Minnesota side. Intermediate.

Location—Distance 45 miles from St. Paul.

Comments—Call Mr. Malmberg for permission and directions to trails he has laid out.

CAMPING UNLIMITED (PRIVATE)

Private camping, cross-country area good for families.

Terrain—Flat to gently rolling country.

Trails—One large loop of about 3 miles, with several cutoffs, easy throughout.

Location—Distance 50 miles from Twin Cities. Take 65 north to Cambridge, go 1 mile west on 95 to County 14. Follow 14 about 6 miles to ski area.

Accommodations—Chalet, sleeping-bag accommodations, and food available to groups only. Contact:

> Camping Unlimited
> Box 392
> Cambridge, Minn. 55008

Comments—Excellent for family skiing.

CROW WING NATURAL HISTORY AREA (PRIVATE)

Private land with interesting wildlife.

Terrain—Open trails, beaver ponds, lakes, meadows.

Trails—Numerous trails of varying lengths, easy.

Location—Distance 140 miles north of Twin Cities via U.S. 169, turn west on 26 just before Garrison (gravel road). Go north from 26 onto 8, to house of caretaker.

Accommodations—Motels in Garrison or Brainerd.

Comments—You must check with caretaker and get permission before using this area!

CANNON RIVER SCOUT CAMP (PRIVATE)

Terrain—River bottoms, wooded.

Trails—Half-a-dozen trails, easy and intermediate, give wide choice of distance.

Location—Distance 50 miles from Twin Cities, near Cannon Falls. South on U.S. 52 to Cannon Falls, west on County 19 to sign CANNON RIVER BOY SCOUT RESERVATION.

Accommodations—Permission to use area must be obtained from:

> Director of Camping
> Indianhead Council, BSA
> 393 Marshall Avenue
> St. Paul, Minn. 55071

This is a group camp, rented for $20 for use of the cabin.

Comments—Cabin has gas plates and electricity, but groups should bring their own cooking equipment.

WISCONSIN

BEAVER VALLEY SCOUT CAMP (PRIVATE)

Scout camp on the St. Croix River near Osceola.

Terrain—Mostly wooded bottomland.

Trails—No established trails, many possible routes. Easy skiing. (Fun drop to camp.)

Location—Distance 40 miles from Twin Cities. Cross river at Stillwater, take Wisconsin 35 through Somerset, turn left at Farmington, left again 1 mile to the Rosenau Farm. Trail to camp to right along fence line across fields.

Accommodations—Primitive cabin. Contact Tom Green. Phone 735-0905.

Comments—Available sometimes to outside groups; usually used weekends by Scouts.

WELCH VILLAGE (PUBLIC)

Trails around downhill ski area, Cannon River banks, and high bluffs. Ski east along railroad tracks to beautiful valley.

Terrain—Flat along river bottoms, rolling hills above the bluffs, steep climb through downhill ski area.

Trails—River-bottom trail one way 2 to 3 miles, easy, starts on north bank of river in town. Hard climb through downhill area to easy rolling country above.

Location—Distance 30 miles southeast of Twin Cities. Take U.S. 35 or 61 south to Highway 50. Go east on 61, 7 miles to the turnoff for Welch Village.

Accommodations—Food available at ski lodge or café in town.

CARLOS AVERY WILDLIFE REFUGE (PUBLIC)

Terrain—Approximately 20 miles long by 4 miles wide. State land, consists of lakes, wooded areas, generally flat with few undulations.

Trails—Roads meander through the preserve; scenery pleasant, in few places frolicking otters may be observed; wildlife abundant.

Location—Take 35-W north, exit State Road 49. Make left, go through Lino Lakes, make left turn, County Road 19. At intersection with County Road 18 turn left, approximately 2 miles, then follow sign to Carlos Avery. Approximately 40 minutes' drive. Many other accesses available.

Accommodations—No shelters.

Comments—May be infested with snowmobiles.

THISTLEDEW LAKE AREA (PUBLIC)

Superb trail system in George Washington State Forest.

Terrain—Rolling hills covered with extensive birch and pine forest.

Trails—There are 15 or more miles of ski trails, mostly well-groomed and signed. Intermediate.

Location—Distance 225 miles due north of Twin Cities. Take U.S. 65 about 24 miles north of Nashwauk, turn left at sign THISTLEDEW LAKE CAMP GROUND. Follow signs for YOUTH CAMP #2 (about 2 miles).

Accommodations—Difficult—best bet is to call Mr. Erling Hegg at 218-376-3783. He can arrange limited accommodations or suggest other camping areas.

Comments—These trails are in regular use by the Department of Corrections Youth Camp, who do a great job of maintenance. The people at the camp are eager to welcome and help skiers.

DEEPWOOD AREA (OPEN)

General ski touring and downhill area around American Youth Hostels (AYH) ski lodge.

Terrain—Open, rolling country, some woods.

Trails—No formally established trails; bring a strong trail-breaker and roll your own.

Location—Near Colfax, 90 miles from Twin Cities. Take U.S. 94 east to Menomonie, go north on 25. Turn right 1 mile north of Wheeler onto County N and follow American Youth Hostels signs.

Accommodations—Shelter and food at the AYH ski lodge; sleeping-bag lodging available. Contact:

Ray Fritz
Deepwood Ski Lodge
Colfax, Wis. 54730
Phone: 715-658-1394

Comments—Good touring area for easy or intermediate skiing.

Telemark Ski Area (Public, Open)

Popular ski area in Wisconsin for downhill, cross-country.

Terrain—Hilly, combining woods and open hills, logging roads.

Trails—No established trails: Forest Lodge Nature Trail near Garmisch Ski Lodge 8 miles east of Cable on County D; North Country Trail on County D, 5 miles south of Grandview. Neither trail has been assessed. Also, unlimited areas for making own trails.

Location—Distance 160 miles from Twin Cities. Take U.S. 8 to Taylors Falls, 63 to Hayward and Cable. Go east on County M to ski area.

Accommodations—Many motels, ski lodges in area, or contact American Youth Hostels, John Jalowitz, Houseparent, Cable, Wis. 54821. Phone: 715-798-3693.

Grantsburg, Wisconsin (Public)

Property of the State of Wisconsin.

Terrain—Generally level, lake and marshland with scrub oak and jack pine, open forest.

Trails—No established trail—do it yourself. Ideal open woods for exploring on skis, with room for several miles of trails, easy.

Location—Distance 80 miles from Twin Cities. Take I-35 to

Pine City, Minnesota, 70 across the St. Croix, take first right turn at top of hill. Area is between the road and the river, south of the highway.

Accommodations—Bring your own lunch. No facilities.

Comments—Free movement and few snowmobiles.

CHICAGO-MILWAUKEE AREA

The Chicago Council of the American Youth Hostels recommends the public trail areas listed below as the best for ski touring in the Chicago-Milwaukee region.

Palos and Sag Valley Forest Preserve:
29 Miles Southwest of Chicago

Easy terrain for cross-country. Ideal for beginners. Thirty-two miles of trails. The most challenging of these is the horse trail running west from the 95th Street service drive intersection just west of Maple Lake. Park at the designated area on the road leading into Bull Frog Lake. The start of the horse trail is hidden from view, 100 yards north. Palos trail map available from Forest Preserve General Headquarters, 536 North Harlem, River Forest, Ill., 60305. Snow information from Palos Headquarters. Tel. 839-5617.

Indiana Dunes State Park:
3 Miles North of Chesterton, Indiana

Excellent trail system. Skiers requested to keep to marked trails and stay off fragile sand hills near Lake Michigan shore. Wooded trails away from the lake hold snow best. Start tour from Wilson Picnic Shelter. Trail map available from the Superintendent, Indiana Dunes State Park, Chesterton, Ind., 46304. Snow information from park. Tel. 926-1215 during business hours.

South Kettle Moraine State Forest:
Southwest of Milwaukee, 110 Miles from Chicago

Superb glacial topography for touring. The following locations are recommended: La Grange Recreation Area: County Highway H, 2 miles north of La Grange, Wis. Good for beginners.

Horseman's Park: County Highway NN, 1 mile southeast of Palmyra, Wis. All the country east to County Highway Z. Challenging. Compass and map needed.

Scuppernong Trail: Circular trail system starts from Forest Headquarters on County Highway ZZ, 1 mile east of Highway 67 (five miles north of Eagle, Wis.). The red trail loop is the easiest.

Ottawa Horse Trail: On County Highway ZZ, .75 mile east of Forest Headquarters. Excellent 4-mile, winding trail loop.

State forest map available from Kettle Moraine State Forest-South Unit, Eagle, Wis., 53119. Snow information from Forest Headquarters during business hours. Tel. 594-2314.

North Kettle Moraine State Forest:
Northwest of Milwaukee, 155 Miles from Chicago

Four circular trails and 26-mile-long Glacial Trail with four open-side Adirondack type overnight shelters. Short tours can be arranged by leaving cars at Crossroads. Glacial Trail between Highways U and V is a very good, up-and-down wooded trail. Leave car at Parnell Lookout Tower parking lot on County Highway U. Trail is .25 mile east.

Circular trails, in order of difficulty from easiest to difficult: Greenbush Trail, several loops from .7 to 4.3 miles; Ray Zilmer Trail, 3.5 miles; Butler Lake Trail, 3.1 miles, western half poor skiing; Parnell Tower Trail, circle loop clockwise, 4 miles. Trail map available from Ice Age Park and Trail Foundation, 735 Water Street, Milwaukee, Wis., 53202. $1.00

donation to foundation will help fund expansion of trail system. Snow information from forest headquarters. Tel. 626-2116. Use caution driving Wisconsin Highway 67 north of Dundee.

Whitnall Park: Hales Corners, Wis.
(Milwaukee Suburb)

Recommend wooded area in north end of park. Start from picnic shelter .5 mile east of park entrance on Highway 100, south of Forest Home Avenue. Snow information available from park. Tel. 425-1133

Blue Mound State Park:
1 Mile Northwest of Blue Mound, Wis.

Moderately hilly terrain.

Blue Mound State Park:
3 Miles South of Ontario, Wis.

Bluff lands; trail system.
Wisconsin snow conditions report available from Department of Natural Resources, Madison, Wis., Thursdays and Fridays. Tel. 608-266-2621. Valuable information from "Visitor's Guide to Wisconsin's State Parks, Forests and Other Recreational Lands" available from the department, Box 450, Madison, Wis., 53701.

Allegan State Game Area:
Near Allegan, Michigan, 150 Miles from Chicago

Extensive, relatively flat area, excellent for beginners. Recommend trails circling Ely Lake and 3-mile cross-country foot trail running east from lake. Trail maps available from Allegan State Game Area, RFD 3, Allegan, Mich., 49010. Snow information from game area headquarters. Tel. 673-2410 during business hours.

MICHIGAN

SYLVANIA TRACT (PUBLIC)

Upper Michigan virgin pines under Forest Service.

Terrain—Gently rolling land under canopy of great virgin pines, hemlock, and birch.

Trails—Two or three trails about 5 miles long, easy to intermediate.

Location—Distance 260 miles northeast of Twin Cities. Take I-35 to U.S. 8, thence to Rhinelander, Wisconsin. Follow Wisconsin 17 to Eagle River, Wisconsin, then U.S. 45 to Watersmeet, Michigan.

Accommodations—Sunset Motel at U.S. 2 and U.S. 45, call 906-358-4550, or Pineaire Motel on U.S. 45, a mile north of Land O' Lakes, Wisconsin, call 906-544-3800. Try Clem's Café at U.S. 2 and U.S. 45, fair. Tulppo's Restaurant in Bruces Crossing good; call ahead.

Comments—A stunning forest, one of the last remaining tracts of virgin forest in the Upper Peninsula, now under Forest's Service's "multiple use" program meaning logging, snowmobiles, etc. Snowmobiles prohibited December 1-February 28.

PORCUPINE MOUNTAINS STATE PARK (PUBLIC)

Michigan State Park in the Upper Peninsula.

Terrain—Mostly forested, hilly country, with some rolling hills and steep drop-offs.

Trails—Numerous major trails, ranging from a very few easy ones to predominantly intermediate and advanced. Use caution on all trails, watch for abrupt turns and steep drops.

Location—Distance 270 miles northeast of Twin Cities.

A class at the Sun Valley Ski School.
Sun Valley Photo

From Ironwood, take U.S. 2 to Wakefield, then 28 to Berglund and 64 to the park.

Accommodations—Food and lodging at the White Pine Inn near the park (906-885-2771); overnight cabins available in the park for about $5 per night.

Comments—Beautiful virgin pine, hemlock, spruce. Good place for winter camping if you are experienced.

IDAHO

Sun Valley in Idaho has entered into the ski-touring activities with a complete program. In addition to cross-country instruction at the ski school, there are weekly NASTAR races. Skijoring adds a new dimension to the sport.

The resort's Nordic program is under the direction of inter-

Cross-country skiing, under the direction of Nordic champion Leif Odmark, was introduced to Sun Valley in 1972. During the season, enthusiasts experience the thrill of gliding over fresh-fallen snow in an atmosphere of tranquility and unsurpassed beauty.

Sun Valley Photo

The annual Reidy Memorial Cross-Country race at Sun Valley.
Sun Valley News Bureau Photo

national champion Leif Odmark. For racers, a variety of courses have been set along the Sun Valley Gold Course. For families and the "tranquil" skier, wide vistas are available in the uninhabited draws north of the resort.

Helicopter tours to nearby ranches offers ski tourers another "different" approach to their activity.

Early-season races at Sun Valley give serious competitors an opportunity to qualify for a national team.

For information, write to:

> Nordic Ski School
> Director, Leif Odmark
> Sun Valley, Idaho 83353

YOSEMITE PROGRAMS FOR TOURERS

Winter activity in the government national parks reflect the considerable swing from Alpine to Nordic skiing. One of the largest ski-touring programs is found in the Yosemite National Park in California. There Yosemite Mountaineering offers a complete spectrum of cross-country and ski mountaineering and tours. A varied program, developed by Yosemite Mountaineering School Director Wayne Merry and veterans of the U.S. Ski Team, provides all levels of instruction from first-day to advanced cross-country, including private coaching for racers. There are one-day ski tours to selected destinations, overnight tours to ski huts, and longer backcountry tours.

The program starts on a weekend basis over Thanksgiving, subject to snow conditions, and daily operations are scheduled from mid-December through early April.

CROSS-COUNTRY INSTRUCTION AT YOSEMITE

The Basic Day: Introduction to cross-country equipment, waxing, basing, single- and double-poling, simple turns, uphill skiing, introduction to hill running. One-day course—$8.

The Intermediate Day: Polishing of above techniques, downhill turns, use of terrain features. Afternoon tour of several miles with frequent instruction stops. Daily—$8.

The Advanced Day: Primarily for the advanced skier or those who learn exceptionally fast the first two days and want to work on the finer points of technique with others of equal ability. Goal is to refine stride and poling, get into basic racing techniques, and generally work toward more personal instruction with smaller classes. One day—$14.

Private Instruction—Racing Coaching: By reservation. Coaching by veterans of U.S. Ski Team for those interested in racing. Special arrangements for college and school teams.

One-day Tours: For those who have received instruction or show capability. Tours are arranged to scenic areas in the park.

The Annual Nordic Cross-Country Race at Yosemite: *Top left*, base preparation before the event; *top right*, one of the youngest entrants; *center*, waiting to go; *bottom*, the race begins.

Photos courtesy Yosemite Park and Curry Company

Every Sunday during the snow season and some holiday weekends—$12.

Children's Classes: Whenever there are enough children between eight and twelve years to form a separate class, they are put together under a selected instructor. Eight is the lowest age for formal classes. The instructors feel that the best way to teach younger children is not to teach formally—just get them on skis and let them get the feel naturally. Children's class, basic or intermediate—$6.

Touring Survival: All persons getting into ski touring are advised to take this survival-oriented tour, which is recommended by the park rangers with the suggestion that "it may save your life." The four- to five-hour course introduces the basics of wilderness navigation, what to take on tours for comfort and survival, how to find the warmest spot in the woods for a forced night out, how to build a fire in a snowstorm, how to make simple, no-tool shelters, how to conserve energy and body heat, and how to aid searchers in finding you. No charge for children eight to twelve. Offered thrice weekly—$8.

Overnight Tours: These are at different levels of skiing and camping ability. Guide fees include breakfast and dinner. A good sleeping bag and warm clothes are required. Prices range from $22 to $60 for a three-day tour.

Special Ski Camping: For the cross-country skiers with basic and intermediate experience and backpacking experience. Designed to provide ski-touring experience with heavy packs and survival and bivouac techniques in the snow. Night is spent in snow caves or other shelter built by participants or in mountain tents—$25.

The Nordic Holiday Weekend: Usually held in March, includes a "fun" 7-mile race for skiers from eight to seventy-five, with a variety of awards. Trail is well marked and of intermediate difficulty.

Other special trips offered through the Yosemite program include air-ski tours to Alaska and trans-Sierra tour.

For detailed information and to make reservations, write to:

Yosemite Park and Curry Co.
Yosemite National Park, Calif. 95389
Tel. 209-372-4671

For information on ski-touring activity in other national parks, write to:

Information Service
National Park Service
Department of the Interior Building
Washington, D.C. 20240

If you are more interested in a specific part of the country, you will find information on ski touring in booklets available from the National Park Service regional offices:

National Capital Regional Office
National Park Service
1100 Ohio Drive, South West
Washington, D.C. 20242

Northeast Regional Office
National Park Service
143 South Third Street
Philadelphia, Pa. 19106

Midwest Regional Office
National Park Service
1709 Jackson Street
Omaha, Neb. 68102

Southeast Regional Office
National Park Service
Federal Building
Box 10008
Richmond, Va. 23240

Southwest Regional Office
National Park Service
Box 728
Santa Fe, N.M. 87501

Western Regional Office
National Park Service
450 Golden Gate Avenue
San Francisco, Calif. 94102

CANADA

QUEBEC

Quebec Parks

The area around Quebec is the center of ski-touring and cross-country activity in Canada. The Viking Ski Club (Box 57, Morin Heights, Quebec) has been in the forefront of activity in this region. In addition, the government of the province has spent well over $3,000,000 to develop cross-country facilities on public lands.

Beaupré

Mont-Sainte-Anne
C.P. 40
Beaupré
(418) 827-4523

Has 10 miles of trails; includes 1 mile beginners; 1 mile intermediate; 1 mile expert; 8 miles wooded trails; 2 miles in open country. Marked trails; cleared trails. Cross-country packages.

Access: R/R 360, 3 miles east of Beaupré.

Magog

Parc du Mont Orford
C.P. 146
Magog
(819) 843-6233
Has 10 miles of trails: 9.5 miles wooded trails; .5 mile in open country.

Mont-Tremblant

Parc du Mont-Tremblant
5075, rue Fullum
Montreal
(810) 688-2833 or (514) 873-2969
Has 60 miles of trails: 3 miles beginners; 5 miles intermediate; 1 mile expert; 55 miles wooded trails; 5 miles in open country.
Access: R/H 15–11, 10 miles from Mont-Tremblant.

Quebec

Parc des Laurentides
Complexe G, 8ᵉ étage
Quebec 4
(418) 643-8774
Has 34 miles of trails: 6 miles beginners; 4 miles intermediate; 3 miles expert; 34 miles wooded trails.
Access; R/H 54, 40 miles north of Quebec.

SOUTHERN QUEBEC

Lac-Megantic

Center Manager, M. Bonin
a/s Pierre Bodard
5561, rue Frontenac
Lac-Megantic

Has 4.5 miles of wooded trails.
Access: R/H 28 and 34.

Mansonville

Owl's Head Ski Area
a/s Fred Korman
Mansonville.
(819) 292-5777
Has 12 miles of wooded trails.
Access: R/H 39.

Sutton-Junction

Mont Echo
a/s André Page
C.P. 458
Knowlton
(514) 243-6722
Has 10 miles of wooded trails.
Access: R/H 39 and 52.

Saint-Daniel

(Frontenac)
Club de Ski de Thetford Mines
a/s Lionel Bourgault
C.P. 261
Thetford Mines
(418) 487-2242, or 335-9157
Has 25 miles of wooded trails.
Access: R/H 1 and 267, 10 miles east of Thetford.

LAURENTIDES–GATINEAU–OUTAOUAIS

Lac-Quenouille

Base de Plein Air

Le P'tit Bonheur
C.P. 30
Lac Carré
(514) 861-8113, or 226-9281
Has 32 miles of trails: 2 miles beginners; 1 mile intermediate; 2 miles expert; 30 miles wooded trails; 2 miles in open country.
Access: R/H 15 and 30.

Lac-Sainte-Marie

Mont Sainte-Marie
John Clifford
Old Chelsea
(819) 467-2848, or 827-1550
Has 3 miles of trails: 1 mile beginners.
Access: R/H 11.

Mont-Tremblant

Mont Tremblant Lodge
a/s Georges Vigeant
Mont-Tremblant
(819) 425-2711
Has 10 miles of trails: 1 mile beginners; 1 mile intermediate; 10 miles wooded trails.
Access: R/H 15 and 11.

Morin Heights

Club de Ski Viking
a/s J. D. Bourne
C.P. 57
Morin Heights
(514) 226-2413
Has 20 miles of trails: including 1 mile beginners; 1 mile intermediate; 1 mile expert; 19 miles wooded trails; 1 mile open country.
Access: R/H 15, 364, 30.

Old Chelsea

Camp Fortune
a/s David Midgley
Old Chelsea
(819) 827-1717

Has 60 miles of trails: includes 2 miles beginners; 7 miles intermediate; 6 miles expert.

Access: R/H 11, 10 miles north of Hull.

Rawdon

Ski Montcalm
350, Chemin du Parc
Rawdon
(514) 834-3139

Has 4 miles of wooded trails.
Access: R/H 25–18.

Sainte-Agathe-des-Monts

Auberge La Calêche
125, tour du Lac
Sainte-Agathe-des-Monts
(819) 326-3753

Offers guided X-C excursions.
Access: R/H 15 and 11.

Saint-Michel-de-Wentworth

Base Sportive Plein Air
C.P. 59
Brownsburg
(514) 226-5892

Has 18 miles of trails; includes 3 miles beginners; 5 miles intermediate; 10 miles wooded trails; 8 miles in open country.

Access: R/H 15, exit 14, R/H 31.

Saint-Sauveur

Mont Habitant
a/s L. Stein, gérant,
Saint-Sauveur
(514) 227-2637

Has 4.5 miles of trails: 3 miles wooded trails; 1.5 miles open country.

Access: R/H 15, exit 26.

Val-David

Hotel La Sapinière
a/s Pierre Verot
Val-David
(819) 322-2020

Has 15 miles of trails.

Access: R/H 11.

Val-Morin

Auberge des Collines
Far Hills Inn
Val-Morin
(514) 866-2219

Has 20 miles of trails: includes 2 miles beginners, 1 mile intermediate; 2 miles expert; 15 miles wooded trails; 5 miles in open country.

Access: R/H 11, 55 miles north of Montreal.

Wakefield

Edelweiss Valley
a/s Andy Tommy
R.R. 2
Wakefield
(819) 459-2386

Has 15 miles of trails: includes 1 mile beginners; 1 mile intermediate; 1 mile expert; 8 miles wooded trails; 7 miles in open country.

Access: R/H 11, 12 miles north of Hull.

MAURICIE–SAINT-MAURICE VALLEY

Grand' Mere

Club de Ski de Fond
Vallee du Parc
Fernand Matteau
641, 7ᵉ rue
Grand'Mere
(819) 538-8628, or 538-9561

Has 13 miles of trails: includes 1 mile beginners; 1 mile intermediate; 1 mile expert; 13 miles wooded trails; 1 mile in open country.

Access: R/H 19.

QUEBEC CITY SKI AREA

Lac-Beauport

Club Oak-Pik
Chateau Lac-Beauport
Lac-Beauport
(418) 849-4468

Has 75 miles of trails: includes 2 miles beginners, 8 miles intermediate; 3 miles expert; 60 miles wooded trails; 15 miles in open country.

Access: R/H 54, 12 miles north of Quebec.

Club Nordic
Auberge Normande
Lac-Beauport
(418) 849-4486

Has 11 miles of trails: 1 mile beginners; 1 mile intermediate; 1 mile expert; 11 miles wooded trails.

Access: R/H 54, 12 miles north of Quebec.

Lac-Delage

Manoir du Lac-Delage
Ville du Lac-Delage
(418) 848-2251

Has 10 miles of trails: 1 mile beginners; 1 mile intermediate; 10 miles wooded trails.

Access: R/H 54, 17 miles north of Quebec.

Lauzon

Centre de Ski de Lauzon
a/s Gilles Boisseau
179, Saint-Antoine
Lévis
(418) 837-7793

Has 20 miles of trails; 1 mile beginners; 2 miles intermediate; 1 mile expert; 5 miles wooded trails; 15 miles in open country.

Access: R/H 2.

Stoneham

Station de Ski de Stoneham
Stoneham
(418) 849-8432

Has 2 miles of trails; 1 mile beginners; 2 miles wooded trails.

Access: R/H 54, 20 miles north of Quebec.

Saint-Adolphe

Le Refuge du Domaine
Saint-Adolphe
Bill Dobson
Saint-Adolphe (Montmorency)
(418) 848-3329

Has 25 miles of trails: includes 3 miles beginners; 3 miles intermediate; 1 mile expert; 25 miles wooded trails.

Access: R/H 54, 22 miles north of Quebec.

SAGUENAY–LAKE SAINT-JEAN

Chambord

Club Mont Dequen
Chambord
(418) 342-6324

Has 2 miles of trails: includes 1 mile beginners; 2 miles wooded trails.

Access: Route 19.

Herbertville

Centre de Plein Air du Mont Lac Vert
C. E. Boudrault
Hôtel de Ville Notre Dame-d'Herbertville
(418) 344-1302

Has 20 miles of trails: 17 miles of wooded trails; 3 miles open country.

Access: R/H 169, 6 miles south of Notre-Dame.

Kenogami

Club de Ski de Fond de Kenogami
a/s André Vallée
8, Boul. des Étudiants
Kenogami
(418) 547-7181

Has 3.5 miles of trails: includes 1 mile intermediate; 3.5 miles wooded trails.

Access: R/H 54, Boul. Taschereau.

Laterrière

Club de Ski de Fond de Chicoutimi
Laterrière
(418) 549-0030, or 549-4530

Has 23 miles of trails: includes 2 miles beginners, 1 mile intermediate; 1 mile expert; 23 miles wooded trails.

Access: R/H 54.

Port-Alfred

Club de Ski Mont Mars
C.P. 34
Port-Alfred
(418) 544-5115, or 544-2331

Has 12 miles of trails: 1 mile beginners; 1 mile intermediate; 1 mile expert; 8 miles wooded trails; 4 miles in open country.

Access: R/H 16.

Saint-Fêlicien

Club de Ski de Fond
Les Sapiniers
a/s Real Lapierre
Saint-Fêlicien
(418) 679-0941, or 679-1946

Has 10 miles of trails; 1 mile beginner; 1 mile intermediate; 1 mile expert; 10 miles of wooded trails.

Access: R/H 169, Notre-Dame Street.

LOWER SAINT-LAURENT AND THE GASPÉ

Base de Plein Air de Matane, Inc.
a/s Rejean Coulombe
C.P. 53
Matane

Has 20 miles of trails; 1 mile beginners; 1 mile intermediate; 1 mile expert; 15 miles wooded trails; 5 miles in open country.

Access: R/N 195, 12 miles from Matane.

Murdochville

Club de Ski de Murdochville
a/s Tom M. Duncan
C.P. 425,
Murdochville
(418) 784-2709, or 784-2908.

Has 7 miles of trails; 7 miles wooded trails.

Access: R/H 198.

Sainte-Blandine

Centre de Ski de Rimouski
Station Val Neigette
a/s Fernand Roy
C.P. 344
Rimouski
(418) 723-1204

Has 10 miles of trails: 8 miles wooded trails; 2 miles in open country.
Access: R/H 232, 9 miles from Rimouski.

Saint-Modeste

Kamouraska
Sentier du Grand Portage
Dr. Jean Bourdeau, president
20, de la Cour
Rivière-du-Loup
(418) 862-5042, or 862-7225

Has 38 miles of trails; 1 mile beginners; 1 mile intermediate; 1 mile expert; 28 miles wooded trails; 10 miles in open country.
Access: R/H 2, 8 miles south of Rivière-du-Loup.

OTHER PARTS OF CANADA

Other parts of Canada have at this writing fallen behind Quebec in the development of ski-touring facilities. However, the growing popularity of trail skiing in Canada has prompted some clubs to begin expanding existing trail systems to accommodate increased memberships and to initiate negotiations with government agencies to utilize park facilities in the wintertime. Most of the present trail systems are maintained by private clubs such as the Ottawa Ski Club's network at Camp Fortune. A limited number of resorts are beginning to stock special ski-touring equipment as a secondary alternative to their Alpine facilities.

In western Canada, many abandoned mining and logging roads are particularly well suited to the Nordic skier.

Current information on ski-touring facilities may be available from the Canadian Government Travel Bureau in Ottawa, Canada, or from any of its fourteen offices in the United States:

Boston, Mass. 02199
263 Plaza
The Prudential Center

Buffalo, N.Y. 14202
1417 Main Place

Chicago, Ill. 60602
100 North LaSalle Street

Cincinnati, Ohio 45202
Room 1010
Enquirer Building
617 Vine Street

Cleveland, Ohio 44115
Winous-Point Building
1250 Euclid Avenue

Detroit, Mich. 48226
Book Building
1257–1259 Washington Blvd.

Los Angeles, Calif. 90014
510 West Sixth Street

Minneapolis, Minn. 55402
124 South Seventh Street
Northstar Center

New York, N.Y. 10019
680 Fifth Avenue

Philadelphia, Pa. 19102
Suite 1309
3 Benjamin Franklin Parkway

Pittsburgh, Pa. 15222
1001–3 Jenkins Arcade
Liberty and Fifth Avenues

San Francisco, Calif. 94104
600 Market Street, Suite 2300
Crocker Plaza

Seattle, Wash. 98101
Suite 1117
Plaza 600
600 Stewart Street

Washington, D.C. 20036
N.A.B. Building
1771 N. Street N.W.

BIBLIOGRAPHY

BRADLEY, DAVIS; MILLER, RALPH; and ALLISON, MERRITT, *Expert Skiing*. New York, Grosset and Dunlap, 1960.

BRADY, M. MICHAEL, *Nordic Touring and Cross-Country Skiing*. Oslo, Dreyers Forlag, 1966.

——, *Nordic Touring and Cross-Country Skiing*, 2d rev. ed. Oslo, Dreyers Forlag, 1970.

CALDWELL, JOHN H., *The Cross-Country Ski Book*. Brattleboro, Vt., Stephen Greene Press, 1964.

CONNERY, D. S., "Lonely Quest in Hapland." *Sports Illustrated*, Vol. 20 (January 27, 1967), pp. 46–47.

ELKINS, FRANK, ed., *The Complete Ski Guide*. New York, Doubleday, Doran & Co., Inc., 1940.

"Falls to Christies." *Recreation*, Vol. 39 (February, 1946), pp. 586–87.

FOSS, WILLIAM, *Skiing*. New York, G. P. Putnam's Sons, 1964.

GORE, H.M., "Next trend in skiing." *Journal of Health, Physical Education and Recreation*, Vol. 12 (February, 1941), pp. 91–92.

HALLBERG, FREDRIK, and MÜCKENBRÜNN, H., *The Complete Book of Ski-ing*. New York, Grunberg, 1936.

HALLBERG, FREDRIK., *Improve Your Skiing*. New York, Dodge Publishing Co., 1936.

HUBER, EDDIE, and ROGERS, NORMAN, *The Complete Ski Manual.* New York, Prentice-Hall, Inc., 1946.

JOHNSON, R. E., "Pre-Season Ski Training." *Journal of Health, Physical Education and Recreation,* Vol. 26 (December, 1955), pp. 8–9.

KINNER, H., "On the Hope of the Snow Gods; Skiing in Norway." *National Review,* Vol. 16 (May 19, 1964), p. 405.

KRAMER, FRANZ, *Ski the New Way.* New York, Sterling Publishing Co., Inc., 1958.

LUND, MORTEN, *The Pleasures of Cross-Country Skiing.* New York, Outerbridge & Lazard, 1972.

LUNN, ARNOLD HENRY MOORE, *Cross-Country Ski-ing.* New York, E. Dutton.

MITCHELL, HAROLD, *Downhill Ski Racing.* New York, Grunberg, 1936.

SWENSON, E., "Let fly downhill." *Harpers,* Vol. 196 (January, 1948), pp. 19–27.

WOOD, S., "Organization of Ski Classes in the College Program." *Journal of Health, Physical Education and Recreation,* Vol. 15 (December, 1944), p. 574.

276

ACKNOWLEDGMENTS

The author wishes to express thanks to the many ski-touring clubs that have cooperated in providing information on this growing winter sport.

The Ski Touring Council has been most helpful in providing data on ski-touring facilities in the eastern United States. The Norwegian Government Information Service has been most helpful with information and photographs. Nordic Ski Promotion of Oslo, Norway provided a wealth of data on equipment and techniques.

The Potomac Appalachian Trail Club of Washington, D.C. provided information on winter camping.

The important information on safety has been provided by the Tacoma Mountain Rescue Unit. The U.S. Army Biathlon Training Unit has provided information on that form of cross-country competition. The United States Olympic Committee has been most helpful in providing information on Olympic competition.

Information on military skiers was provided by the Office of the Chief of Information, Department of the Army.

The North Star Ski Touring Club of Minneapolis provided data on touring facilities in its part of the country. The Tourist Office of the Canadian Government provided information on ski-touring facilities in Canada.

The bibliography was prepared by Gerald F. Davis, librarian, Babson Library of Springfield College, Springfield, Massachusetts.

Waxing tips courtesy the SWIX Ski Wax Company.

277

INDEX

280

281

282